P9-DEM-922

CRITICAL THEMES IN WORLD MUSIC

Critical Themes in World Music is a reader of nine short essays by the authors of the successful *Excursions in World Music*, Eighth Edition, edited by Timothy Rommen and Bruno Nettl. The essays introduce key and contemporary themes in ethnomusicology—gender and sexuality, coloniality and race, technology and media, sound and space, and more—creating a counterpoint to the area studies approach of the textbook, a longstanding model for thinking about the musics of the world. Instructors can use this flexible resource as a primary or secondary path through the materials, on its own, or in concert with *Excursions in World Music*, allowing for a more complete understanding that highlights the many continuities and connections that exist between musical communities, regardless of region. *Critical Themes in World Music* presents a critically-minded, thematic study of ethnomusicology, one that serves to counterbalance, complicate, and ultimately complement the companion textbook.

Timothy Rommen is the Davidson Kennedy Professor in the College and Professor of Music and Africana Studies at the University of Pennsylvania.

TO THE MEMORY OF BRUNO NETTL (1930–2020)

I continue to believe that fundamentally, despite differences in complexity and technology, all musics are equal, equally valuable.

"Have You Changed Your Mind?
Reflections on Sixty Years in Ethnomusicology"
(*Acta Musicologica*, 2017).

CRITICAL THEMES IN WORLD MUSIC

A Reader for *Excursions in World Music*,
Eighth Edition

Edited by
Timothy Rommen

*Marié Abe, Andrea F. Bohlman, Richard Jankowsky,
Joshua D. Pilzer, Chérie Rivers Ndaliko, Lei Ouyang,
and Jim Sykes*

Routledge
Taylor & Francis Group

NEW YORK AND LONDON

First published 2021
by Routledge
52 Vanderbilt Avenue, New York, NY 10017

and by Routledge
2 Park Square, Milton Park, Abingdon, Oxon, OX14 4RN

Routledge is an imprint of the Taylor & Francis Group, an informa business

© 2021 Taylor & Francis

The rights of Timothy Rommen to be identified as the author
of the editorial material, and of Marié Abe, Andrea F. Bohlman,
Richard Jankowsky, Joshua D. Pilzer, Chérie Rivers Ndaliko, Lei Ouyang,
and Jim Sykes for their individual chapters, has been asserted in accordance
with sections 77 and 78 of the Copyright, Designs and Patents Act 1988.

All rights reserved. No part of this book may be reprinted or reproduced or
utilised in any form or by any electronic, mechanical, or other means, now
known or hereafter invented, including photocopying and recording, or in
any information storage or retrieval system, without permission in writing
from the publishers.

Trademark notice: Product or corporate names may be trademarks or
registered trademarks, and are used only for identification and explanation
without intent to infringe.

Library of Congress Cataloging-in-Publication Data
Names: Rommen, Timothy, editor. | Abe, Marie, contributor. | Bohlman,
Andrea F., contributor. | Jankowsky, Richard, contributor. | Pilzer,
Joshua D., contributor. | Ndaliko, Chérie Rivers, contributor. |
Ouyang, Lei, contributor. | Sykes, Jim, contributor.
Title: Critical themes in world music : a reader for Excursions in world
music, eighth edition / Timothy Rommen, Marie Abe, Andrea F.
Bohlman, Richard Jankowsky, Joshua D. Pilzer, Cherie Rivers
Ndaliko, Lei Ouyang, Jim Sykes.
Description: New York : Routledge, 2020. | Includes bibliographical
references and index.
Identifiers: LCCN 2020012643 (print) | LCCN 2020012644 (ebook) |
ISBN 9781138354562 (hardback) | ISBN 9781138354609 (paperback) |
ISBN 9780429424717 (ebook)
Subjects: LCSH: Ethnomusicology. | World music--History and criticism.
Classification: LCC MT90 .E95 2020a (print) | LCC MT90 (ebook) |
DDC 780.9--dc23
LC record available at https://lccn.loc.gov/2020012643
LC ebook record available at https://lccn.loc.gov/2020012644

ISBN: 978-1-138-35456-2 (hbk)
ISBN: 978-1-138-35460-9 (pbk)
ISBN: 978-0-429-42471-7 (ebk)

Typeset in Galliard
by Servis Filmsetting Ltd, Stockport, Cheshire

CONTENTS

ABOUT THE AUTHORS

Timothy Rommen studied at the University of Chicago and has, since 2002, taught at the University of Pennsylvania. Working primarily in the Caribbean, his research interests include coloniality/decoloniality, the political economy of music and sound, creole musical formations, tourism, diaspora, music and religion, and the ethics of style. He is the author of *"Funky Nassau": Roots, Routes, and Representation in Bahamian Popular Music*, and *"Mek Some Noise": Gospel Music and the Ethics of Style in Trinidad*.

Marié Abe studied at the University of California, Berkeley and teaches at Boston University. Working primarily in Japan, the US, and Ethiopia, her research interests include the politics of sound and public space, affect, social precarity, as well as the intersection of music, violence, social movements, and the everyday. She also likes to play the accordion, which helps her to think about issues of migration, diasporic formations, colonialism, and circulation. She is the author of *Resonances of Chindon-ya: Sounding Space and Sociality in Contemporary Japan*.

Andrea F. Bohlman studied at Harvard University and teaches at the University of North Carolina, Chapel Hill. Her research on music, sound, and social movements in eastern and central Europe was recently published in a book, *Musical Solidarities: Political Action and Music in Late Twentieth-Century Poland*. She has additional interests in listening and media, especially tape recording; migration and mobilities; nationalisms and dissent; emotion and environment; and memory work. She also writes on the Eurovision Song Contest.

Richard Jankowsky studied at the University of Chicago and teaches at Tufts University. His research interests include music of North Africa and the Middle East, trance and healing, ritual and religion, and rhythmic theory. He is the author of *Stambeli: Music, Trance, and Alterity in Tunisia*; and editor of *The Continuum Encyclopedia of Popular Musics of the World: Genres of the Middle East and Africa*.

Joshua D. Pilzer studied at the University of Chicago and teaches at the University of Toronto. His research interests include the relationships between music, sound, voice, survival, memory, traumatic experience, marginalization, gendered violence, everyday life, and identity. He is the author of *Hearts of Pine: Songs in the Lives of Three Korean Survivors of the Japanese "Comfort Women,"* and is currently finishing another ethnographic book on the musicality of everyday life among Korean victims of the atomic bombing of Japan and their children.

Chérie Rivers Ndaliko studied at Harvard University and teaches at the University of North Carolina at Chapel Hill. She also serves as director of research and education at Yole!Africa in Goma, DRC. Building on decolonial and subaltern perspectives, her research and activism on expressive culture, epistemology, and ecology seek to subvert global systems of power. Her books include *Necessary Noise: Music, Film, and Charitable Imperialism in the East of Congo* and *The Art of Emergency: Aesthetics and Aid in African Crises.*

Lei Ouyang studied at the University of Pittsburgh and has, since 2017, taught at Swarthmore College where she co-directs the Chinese Music Ensemble. She previously taught at Skidmore College and Macalester College. Her research interests include memory, politics, race and ethnicity, and social justice. She has conducted fieldwork in the United States, Japan, People's Republic of China, and Taiwan. She is the author of the forthcoming book *Music as Mao's Weapon: Songs and Memories of the Chinese Cultural Revolution.*

Jim Sykes studied at the University of Chicago and teaches at the University of Pennsylvania. His research interests include music, religion, personhood, modernity, and the politics of disaster in the Indian Ocean region, with a focus on Sri Lanka and Singapore. He is the author of *The Musical Gift: Sonic Generosity in Post-War Sri Lanka* and coeditor with Gavin Steingo of *Remapping Sound Studies.*

PREFACE

This reader is designed to accompany the eighth edition of *Excursions in World Music*. This new reader includes an introduction and eight chapters on themes that are central to ethnomusicological inquiry. These include:

- *Music, Gender, and Sexuality*
- *Music and Ritual*
- *Coloniality and World Music*
- *Music and Space*
- *Music and Diaspora*
- *Communication, Technology, Media*
- *Musical Labor, Musical Value*
- *Music and Memory*

For Students

Each short chapter (approx. 4,000 words) introduces you to the theme at hand and then illustrates it with reference to musical examples drawn from at least three chapters of *Excursions in World Music*. In so doing, the reader becomes a way for you to engage with the musics of the world thematically as well as from the area studies perspective presented in the textbook. The new reader, too, should be considered a major resource for generating deeper engagement with and understanding of the musical practices and communities that you read about in the textbook. Your instructor may choose to assign only a few chapters from the reader to augment thematically the goals of the course, but it is equally possible to use the reader as the first point of entry into materials in the textbook. However the reader is integrated into your classroom experience, it is my hope that you'll explore all of the short chapters in order to get a better sense of the enduring concerns and political stakes that animate ethnomusicological inquiry.

For Instructors

Instructors can use this reader as a primary or secondary path through the materials. Having available both an area studies and a thematic approach to the materials offers important pedagogical flexibility and also provides students with additional means of engaging with the musics of the world. This thematic reader can be integrated into your course plans in any number of ways. Instructors could choose to introduce students to a chapter from the textbook and then augment their engagement with that material by assigning a chapter from the reader that connects, in its examples, to that chapter. Conversely, instructors could decide to engage a broad theme (such as gender and sexuality, or music and memory) first, and then follow the examples offered in the reader to the chapters in the textbook for further study. The goal here is to offer multiple paths through the material, such that those instructors more comfortable teaching thematically have a strong set of essays to help organize such an approach while still connecting directly to the textbook. But, for those instructors who prefer the area studies approach of the textbook, the reader offers a set of additional readings to generate more depth, opportunity for classroom discussion, and thematic focus for a few units within a given semester.

The authors have all contributed essays to this reader with the aim of ensuring that both students and instructors have at their disposal a rich set of resources for negotiating the many musics of the world and the equally rich set of critical themes that emerge as scholars explore the communities within which these sounds are produced. Just as many instructors will not use all chapters of *Excursions in World Music* during a given semester, so too, the reader is designed for maximum flexibility. The chapters are not ordered consecutively, nor should instructors feel that students need to read all of them in order to productively integrate the reader into their course—they can be assigned in any order, and in any proportion. It is my sincere hope that instructors will find the reader a welcome and useful addition to this new edition of *Excursions in World Music*.

Timothy Rommen
Philadelphia, Spring 2020

1

INTRODUCTION

Timothy Rommen

Music is powerful: it can provide the soundtrack for protest ("We Shall Overcome," Black Lives Matter); it drives or accompanies rituals of all sorts (religious services, healing ceremonies, coronations); it can be mobilized for propaganda (Chinese "Songs for the Masses"); it can trigger memories of places, emotions, tastes, and smells ("Auld Lang Syne," that slow-dance tune from Prom); it helps us produce solidarities (college team fight songs, indie concerts); it affects our mood (makes our workout more intense, helps us relax at the beach); it is used as a marketing tool (advertising jingles, elevator music); and it drives us to move (whether in the club, at a concert, or in our own living rooms). Music accompanies us through life ("Happy Birthday," weddings, children's songs), animating much of what we do and contributing to our sense of self (playlists, fandom). It is, in fact, so ubiquitous that we could be forgiven if we sometimes take its power for granted in our everyday lives.

But what if we really pay attention to music? What if we listen carefully for what we can hear, discover, and come to understand through sound? One of the aims of the discipline of ethnomusicology is to engage deeply with sound and music in order to come to a better understanding of what it means to be human, what it means to live in community, and what it means to make social and political meaning through sound. As a discipline rooted in the humanities but drawing methodologically from the social sciences (and anthropology, in particular), ethnomusicology has a lot to offer to those who are interested in these big ideas and in how they can help us "hear" power, or subjectivity, or memory, among many other possibilities.

Area Studies?

This short reader, designed to accompany your textbook, *Excursions in World Music*, aims to introduce you to some of the critical themes that occupy ethnomusicology in the contemporary moment. In so doing, it creates a counterpoint with a rather longstanding model for thinking about the musics of the world within the discipline of ethnomusicology itself. Let me explain: your textbook, *Excursions in World Music*, is organized according to a logic that

1

was very prevalent throughout the US academy in the mid- to late-twentieth century—that is to say, it is organized around the idea of area studies. Although thinking about music in Maritime Southeast Asia or the Middle East is, without doubt, one productive way to present some of the musics of the world, it goes without saying that there are also significant drawbacks to such an organizational structure. For starters, it can inadvertently suggest a homogeneity within regions that is not ever as stable or complete as it may seem. A regional approach also makes it harder to highlight the many continuities and connections that exist *between* musical communities that happen to live in different "regions." Charting musical migrations or the sounds of shared waterways is just harder to accomplish within an area studies model.

The important thing to understand about area studies is that it grew out of US cold war policy, which dictated that understanding the languages, histories, and cultural practices of those regions not yet aligned with the US or the Soviet Union would be key to the continued spread of democracy (and with it the expansion of US interests and influence). The connection to ethnomusicology (and, by extension, to your textbook) is that significant resources were poured into universities for the purpose of establishing Area Studies Centers—a turn of events that had dramatic effects on what it was possible to study and how such study was structured. Studying cultural areas, thus, became something that anthropologists and ethnomusicologists did, and it also became something that they trained their students to do. Structuring courses and textbooks around regions was a fairly straightforward application of this approach within curricula, and *Excursions in World Music* is a good example of this model.

I mention this historical context here because ethnomusicologists, like scholars in many other disciplines, must be clear-eyed about the lasting impact of what has been called the colonial matrix of power (Quijano 2000). What I mean here is that the academy itself bears within its own structures of thought and institutional practices the intellectual biases and economic benefits of the long colonial project (and area studies is but one concrete example of this project). What counts as knowledge? Who gets to decide what is valued and what is not? What is taught and what is not? Who decides where resources are spent?

This reader offers an opportunity to reflect on how answers to these questions can offer a foundation for drawing the best from the past while guarding against any uncritical assumption that current scholarship is somehow "superior." For example, this reader is organized along a more contemporary approach revolving around theme, not region, but this approach, too, has drawbacks. Privileging themes instead of regions can, for example, inadvertently draw equivalencies across rather incommensurate musical practices and communities. It can also pay insufficient attention to those musical practices that complicate or only partially connect with a particular theme but are, nevertheless, crucial to arriving at a balanced understanding.

There are good reasons, then, to preserve a critically informed area studies or regional model of presentation and to pair it with an equally critically-minded thematic one. These approaches counterbalance and complicate one another and it is in this spirit that you should engage with this reader. As you read the chapters in your textbook, you'll notice that many authors have chosen to take a thematic approach to their regional coverage, doing a bit of this kind of work even within each chapter. Each chapter in the reader inverts this presentation of materials and ideas, introducing a crucial theme that is then illustrated with reference to three or four musical examples drawn from several different chapters in *Excursions in World Music*. In so doing, the goal is to connect both modes of presentation and thus highlight their strengths.

World Music?

Before thinking a bit more specifically about the aims of this reader and the chapters themselves, I'd like to briefly explore one more history—the history of World Music, a concept that appears in the titles of both your textbook and this reader. In fact, you can think of this as the first "critical theme" to which this reader is dedicated. World Music is a convenient catch-all term for musics that fall outside of the North Atlantic (primarily Anglophone) popular music industry. As such, it can offer a way of grouping together many of the musics of the world. It is also an industry term that has spawned recording labels, festivals, and tours, mostly owned, organized, and operated by North Atlantic (read White) interests. And yet, it is also a term that, since the 1980s, when it started to be used, has been both exceedingly opaque and incredibly confining/constricting/delimiting for those artists who find themselves characterized as "world musicians."

Opaque because it makes no distinction between art musics, traditional practices, and popular musics. Leaving aside, for the moment, the difficulty of arriving at any satisfactory definition of these categories in the first place, it is clear that Hindustani music, joiks, and soca are better thought of as distinct practices rather than grouped together as examples of "World Music." A category this capacious ultimately loses all coherence and explanatory power. Confining/constricting/delimiting because, once categorized and marketed as "world musicians," artists are separated from the North Atlantic music industry, and this despite the fact that many of these musicians are deeply invested in genres that could easily count as more intimately connected to the North Atlantic music industry than they are to "World Music." For instance, how do we think about Hip Hop in Ghana or Senegal? R&B or Indie music in India? World Music is, in these cases, revealed as a market category that confines artists in ways that their practice obviously and consistently transcends.

World Music is also yet another example of the colonial matrix of power in the contemporary moment. As articulated by cultural brokers, intellectuals, and the industry, what counts as art music is, in fact, Western Classical music, and not Hindustani music or Javanese Gamelan, or the many other art musics the world over. Those practices are conveniently relegated to the category of World Music. What counts as popular music, moreover, is sung mostly in English and produced in and disseminated from the North Atlantic. This means that "popular musics" such as Dangdut, or Cumbia, or Soukous, are relegated to the same category—World Music. The same principle holds for traditional musics of the "West" versus those from the rest of the world. And this deeply flawed and colonially-informed logic isn't just an industry issue. It is translated directly into the academy by means of courses like "Introduction to World Music" or through courses that focus on popular music, or art music, but take for granted that the terrain upon which such courses are built incorporates only the North Atlantic.

The continuing coloniality of World Music has been clear to many within the industry and the academy for many years. As just one example of this, David Byrne (of Talking Heads fame), wrote a stinging article for the *New York Times*, entitled "I Hate World Music" (Oct 3, 1999), in which he bluntly assessed the issues I've been outlining here. He wrote:

> In my experience, the use of the term world music is a way of ... relegating this "thing" into the realm of something exotic and therefore cute, weird but safe, because exotica is beautiful but irrelevant; they are, by definition, not like us. Maybe that's why I hate the term. It groups everything and anything that isn't "us" into "them" ... It's a none too subtle way of reasserting the hegemony of Western pop culture. It ghettoizes most of the world's music. A bold and audacious move, White Man!

So, we would all do well to approach an album, a course, a textbook, or a reader (like this one), that proposes to deal with World Music with a healthy dose of skepticism. And yet, the term World Music also offers us an opportunity to think about how, even as we acknowledge the challenges and difficulties of the term, we can confront the state of the industry and the academy and then begin to unpack what we can learn about the musics of the world when we step outside of this category. In other words, holding World Music in a critical light offers a starting point for undoing its legacies and logics. So, I'd like to suggest that continuing to address ourselves to a concept like World Music allows us to problematize its assumptions, to hold it in tension with the many other ways we might categorize the musics of the world, and to reveal something of the ongoing specters of coloniality that continue to structure our experiences and even our curricular options.

Critical Themes

Let's now turn our attention to thinking about the aims of this companion reader. Perhaps we should start with a few questions. Why study music at all? What can we learn from listening to and thinking about the musics of the world that we couldn't learn better through attending to other subjects? How does music afford us access to ways of thinking and being not easily addressed in other ways? In order to answer these questions, I'll touch briefly on four broad categories within which thinking through sound and music can provide particular insight.

Music and Encounter

Ethnomusicology is a discipline that relies methodologically on fieldwork and ethnography. As such, one of the distinguishing features of this discipline is the privileged place accorded to encounters of all sorts. These encounters often take place between ourselves and the musicians, producers, listeners, and other interlocutors we work with in the field, but they can also involve our experiences with new ideas about music or new perspectives on history, to name but two of many possibilities. As we engage with our interlocutors, then, our encounters can include a wide range of experiences, including confronting difference, or discovering histories of deep connection. Our encounters can help us work toward understanding patterns of musical life that revolve around diaspora, or migration, or exile. Encounters also offer us a foundation from which to wrestle with the obvious legacies of coloniality in the communities we work among and a starting point for our attempts to come to terms with histories of violence and trauma. Our encounters with technology also shape our relationship to sound and music, both in terms of how we listen, and also in thinking about media flows and the mechanics of sound production, recording, and distribution.

One of the things that the authors of all the chapters in this reader share is a deep commitment to thinking *with* individuals and their communities. And, as you can imagine, encounters with our fellow world citizens are bound up in very important considerations around power relationships, the politics of representation, and questions of reciprocity. All of these concerns around how best to approach our encounters in the field and our responsibilities and obligations after we return "home," moreover, are part of the next category we need to consider—ethics.

Music and Ethics

Ethnomusicologists face a set of ethical issues in the course of our work. Each and every time we venture to explore a new project, revisit old friends and interlocutors, or decide to publish our findings in journals or as films, we need to consider the ethics of our actions. So let's think just briefly about the three areas I mentioned above. You are likely familiar with power relationships in your own experience. Some of them are fairly commonplace: when you were in middle school you likely tried to respect your teachers, because they might have given you a detention if you didn't; or maybe you were someone's supervisor at the job you worked at in high school, in which case you may have had a bit of power over their work schedule or raises? You've also likely encountered situations in which gender dynamics revealed underlying power differentials? Think here of certain forms of male privilege and entitlement (mansplaining, for instance). In all of these cases, there is the potential for those with more power in a given relationship to abuse that in some way.

In the case of ethnomusicologists, these power relationships are somewhat more complex. We are often in unfamiliar places, beholden to our interlocutors for guidance and kindnesses as we figure out how to get around and get used to things. And yet, we are also often only temporary residents in these places (a semester or two, thanks to a grant), have the ability to return to our university campuses or research centers, benefit from a certain freedom of mobility and access afforded to us by our affiliations (both national and institutional), and have other forms of power to which our local interlocutors may not have access. Cultivating an awareness of how we are relating in these situations, and developing a vigilance about the explicit and implicit power relationships at play in any given context are thus crucial to our ability to foster equitable and ethical relationships in the course of our fieldwork.

As a rule, ethnomusicologists tend to be strong advocates for the people, musics, and cultures they study—people, musics, and cultures which have often experienced long histories of exclusion or marginalization within North Atlantic academia. And yet, we also tend to be members of university communities, and we are often researching and writing for a living (that is, we are producing dissertations, and then articles, films, and books from the encounters we have in the "field") and must therefore negotiate additional ethical questions in the process of translating our encounters with our interlocutors into texts largely consumed by the scholarly community. These questions and concerns we can group under the rubric of the politics of representation. Who speaks? Who has the power to dictate the narrative or storylines? Who gets to decide what gets left out? There are many ways of addressing these concerns, such as: co-authoring sections of or whole documents with our interlocutors; circulating drafts of our work and then engaging with our interlocutors' responses to it; or, creating multiple "products/texts" and making them more accessible to the communities we work with through online repositories, photo essays, films, or oral history projects. All of these strategies for addressing the politics of representation fall under the category of reciprocity. That is, what can we do to give even as we receive in these encounters?

Music and/as Performance

And this brings me to the third category that broadly defines the work of ethnomusicologists. We are, as a group, alive to the possibilities of performance—and this both in terms of our own relations (to the "field"; to our interlocutors; to our institutions; to ourselves) and with regard to the everyday performances we witness during our encounters. Many of us play music, dance, record, compose, or otherwise engage in such performances as we work in and among the communities we encounter. We also regularly explore questions such as what gesture and the body, gender and sexuality, and the performances related to childhood, or aging, or affect, can teach us about the nature of performance. There are opportunities here for reciprocity, to be sure, even as there are significant theoretical and critical possibilities to be pursued.

It is through our performances (as researchers, musicians, dancers, etc.) that we also leave traces of our presence and encounters in the field (how could we not?). As one textbook on ethnographic methods phrases it, we leave "shadows in the field" (Barz and Cooley 2008). But I'd like to suggest that these traces, if grounded in shared, ethical, and reciprocal relationships, can be much more than mere shadows, for they are made up of our own performances in the act of encounter; of our own performances as we negotiate power relationships; of our own performances vis-à-vis the politics of representation; and of our own performances of reciprocity.

Music and Memory

A final category that animates ethnomusicologists can be summed up by the term memory, by which I mean histories (both written and oral), traditions, myths, rituals, nostalgias, and all the stuff that informs the stories we tell about ourselves and the myriad ways that we perform those in the contemporary moment. What can music tell us about those stories? How can music help tell them? What new questions emerge when we "listen" for memory? What silences do we encounter? How were they produced and by whom? And what do they mean? Much of what we wind up writing (or editing into film) is deeply engaged with many of these forms of memory, and music consistently offers us a means of exploring these from an artistic and intellectual perspective. Often "listening" to ritual, or myth, or history through sound and music can generate insights and nuances otherwise difficult to access. It is also the case that music is often produced by communities whose performances of memory challenge, subvert, or otherwise push back against official narratives and common wisdom. For all of these reasons, ethnomusicologists attend carefully to the ways that music connects us to memory.

This Reader

The chapters in this reader offer an introduction to several themes that ethnomusicologists continue to think about. In a series of eight short chapters, the authors (who have also authored the chapters of your textbook, *Excursions in World Music*) outline the political stakes of these themes, demonstrate the kind of thinking through sound that these themes make possible, and illustrate these possibilities with reference to musical examples drawn from several chapters of your textbook. I introduce the topics here, very schematically, just to give you a sense for what's ahead. But even as I do so, you'll notice that you could easily extend this list yourself. As with any such effort, this reader offers a selective and necessarily partial statement, but I hope it will be useful to you and spur your own thinking about the power of music and the reasons why thinking with sound can be so rewarding.

Chapter 2, written by Joshua D. Pilzer, concerns itself with the many ways that music can help us explore, nuance, and problematize questions related to **Music, Gender, and Sexuality**. Josh encourages us to wrestle with the ways that gender and sexuality are, at one and the same time, normalized and contested through musical performance. Music, in other words, offers both conservative and radical possibilities in this regard. Chapter 3, authored by Richard Jankowsky, takes us on a journey through the various registers in which **Music and Ritual** operate around the world. Rich helps us think about three powerful registers within which music and ritual are mobilized: at the level of healing and trance, in connection with the state and public spectacle, and in the act of listening as individuals or in groups.

Chapter 4, contributed by Chérie Rivers Ndaliko, wrestles with the history of **Coloniality and "World Music"** and the more recent possibilities afforded by decolonial projects, thinking in particular about how musical performance offers us the opportunity to begin to name the histories of domination and the violences accompanying colonial projects. But she also helps us to imagine the terrain upon which truly decolonial projects can be articulated and the ways in which musicians have already shown us the way. Marié Abe, in Chapter 5, offers a meditation on **Music and Space**, giving us a glimpse into the multifarious ways that space can be thought and made meaningful through musical performance. She helps us think about how music has been used to reinforce and challenge absolute space, about how music and space has been theorized within phenomenology, and about what happens when we think of music and space as relational, emergent, and connected to the more-than-human.

Chapter 6, entitled **Music and Diaspora** and written by Timothy Rommen, explores the patterns, challenges, and possibilities that diasporic communities face and how music can offer insights into these dynamics. This chapter offers an exploration of classic instances of diaspora, with examples drawn from the African diaspora, and then opens onto the musical lives of more recently displaced people and migrant communities in order to think about what music can provide and mean in such circumstances. Andrea F. Bohlman, who contributes Chapter 7, helps us gain insight into the relationship between **Communication, Technology, Media,** and music. Andrea is interested in helping us understand the everyday realities of our musical engagements and the ways these are mediated through technology. But she is also deeply invested in getting us to think about how technology, media, and communication actively shape the meanings that music accrues as it is disseminated.

Chapter 8, authored by Jim Sykes, explores the notions of **Musical Labor** and **Musical Value** in global perspective. In this chapter, Jim illustrates how very differently musical value and musical labor are conceptualized as we explore examples from different communities around the world. A final chapter, entitled **Music and Memory** and written by Lei Ouyang, helps us think about how powerfully music and memory are linked. She introduces us to several paired terms that help explore this theme, including: performer and listener, individual and collective, content and process, and past and present. As each of these sections unfolds, Lei builds an increasingly nuanced and rich framework for thinking about the dynamic relationship between music and memory.

There is no doubt that many "critical themes" could be added to this collection of essays. For instance, it would be wonderful to include a chapter on music and the everyday, or a chapter on music, violence, and trauma, or a chapter engaged with music and disability, or childhood. It would be fabulous, moreover, to consider music and social justice, or music and Indigenous rights, or music and the environment, and perhaps future editions of this reader will do just that. But, as I pointed out at the beginning of this Introduction, one of the aims of the discipline of ethnomusicology is to engage deeply with sound and music in order to come to a better understanding of what it means to be human, what it means to live in community, and what it means to make social and political meaning through sound. The chapters that are included here are a step toward doing just that—toward understanding the power of music to help us intervene in, nuance, and explore issues that concern us all. It is my hope that you will encounter in the pages that follow roadmaps and prompts for engaging meaningfully with sound and music, and consistent encouragement to think about what music might reveal not only about yourself, but also about the communities you are connected to, and perhaps even about all of us.

References

Barz, Gregory and Timothy J. Cooley. 2008. *Shadows in the Field: New Perspectives for Fieldwork in Ethnomusicology*. 2nd edition. New York: Oxford University Press.

Quijano, Aníbal. 2000. "Coloniality of Power and Eurocentrism in Latin America." *International Sociology* 15/2: 215–232.

2

MUSIC, GENDER, AND SEXUALITY

Joshua D. Pilzer

Excursions in World Music is filled with examples of music's role in the creation and maintenance of selfhood and identity. These identities may be national, they may concern ideas about race, class, place, era, or other things. But they are as typically based, if not more so, in notions of gender and sexuality. Ask yourself: what percentage of the songs you know are about love? If they are about love, they are likely about people who love; and they propagate ideas about *who* should love *whom*, and *how*. There are many other ways that music can be about gender and sexuality, but the love song is rather a central one.

Imagine a country singer who identifies as a heterosexual man, who wakes up to discover he is no longer Texan, but Australian. He might struggle with the Vegemite and other things, but within a relatively short time he would have settled down to being an Australian country singer. Now imagine instead that he woke up a Texan woman, or a trans woman, or a gay man. How much harder would it be to put on those hats? And what would she/he sing then? Yes, some of our identities, however precious we claim them to be, would be more easily shifted than others. Gender and sexual identities are perhaps the two that most people cling to the most urgently, often violently, and rehearse most earnestly in musical performance, often without realizing it.

There are several reasons why music gets called up for the delicate work of managing gendered and sexual identities. First of all, music, like many other expressive arts, is based in performance, and it puts the body on the line. Performing bodies and voices are put on stages, screens, and recordings; and these voices and bodies become recognizable types of the basic categories of culture—women, men, children, others—and perform relationships between them. Music becomes a means of teaching people what gendered and sexual identities are sanctioned and which are not. And it becomes, at the same time, a place where the rules of this propriety are contested, transgressed, suspended, and reworked.

Second, music is a cultural resource for the working out and the socialization of gendered and sexual identities because it has a malleability that suits it to expressing these fluid concepts of culture. Music is, except for in the most extreme instances, characterized by plasticity and flexibility, no matter how people may try to pin it down or rationalize it. Even the most austere, canonized,

10

and worshipped musics the world over, which are assumed to be preserved and transmitted without alteration, change radically over time, and even from performance to performance.

Take a moment to consider the fluidity of gender and sexuality in unexpected places. An example: you are listening to a well-known pop-country song in which an unspecified man, assumed to be the singer, hops on horseback and rides into a large city, hoots at pretty "girls" (women, we hope), and is met with the titular reply from these women: "Save a Horse, Ride a Cowboy!" This song, sung by two men, seems to present an aggressively simple, heterosexual version of love, or perhaps just sex, or perhaps just masculinity, and love and sex and women are only important as foils for that masculinity. So why would the protagonist ride a horse in an act of male mastery, only to turn around and become the mastered horse?

Most people grow up urged to take certain sexes, genders and sexualities for granted, and to consider others abhorrent. And yet even in this song, with such conventional notions of gender and sexuality in the air, love, sex, gender, and sexuality are not straightforward in the least. They are messy and nuanced to a degree, and above all they are mobile (de Beauvoir 1953). That is why states, societies, and cultures—including musical ones—expend such energy and inflict such violence in efforts to make it seem otherwise. But it is also a reason why there are so many love songs, and why so many people marginalized by these fictions and their violences take refuge in music and dance.

From the beginnings of ethnomusicology, scholars have encountered a range of gender roles that has made it impossible to believe that there are only two "natural" genders, male and female. Indigenous peoples of North America and the Pacific have long made space in culture for third and fourth genders—people assigned female at birth who occupy the roles of men, and vice versa, nowadays referred to by the shorthand "two spirited." There are numerous other examples of third and fourth genders in South Asia, Southeast Asia, and elsewhere. Almost all these peoples were victims of colonial criminalization, marginalization, "conversion therapies," and other horrors. In addition to this, even in cultures that have binary conceptions of gender, the concepts of "woman" and "man" are radically different around the world. In traditional Korea, for instance, a male person only became a "man" at marriage, and unmarried males of any age were considered boys. For these reasons **the social sciences distinguish *sex*, referring to chromosomal, hormonal, and anatomical sexual characteristics, and *gender*, referring to a social role, as distinct entities**. Humanity's general, although far from absolute, tendency to two sets of sexual characteristics, called *sexual dimorphism*, does not map automatically onto two genders. That so many people believe it does is a measure of how much effort patriarchal societies have put into trying to stamp out the gender diversity of our world in the interest of further consolidating their own power.

11

Musical Constructions/Articulations of
Gender and Sexuality

Sex is a matter of biology; but it is quite complex, involving chromosomes, hormones, and anatomy that often diverge from one another and spread out into continua which link poles of so-called female and male sex characteristics. This complexity makes it quite reasonable to consider the enforcement of sexual dimorphism as natural law and processes of sex assignment to be functions of gender ideology. Gender, by contrast, is entirely socially constructed. This is quite different from saying it is a fiction; it is no less real than anything else people make. What it does mean, however, is that there are observable, historical processes by which genders come to be, and that they can be witnessed "under construction," maintenance, and remodeling in the moment. This is because gender is constantly being *performed* (see Butler 1988); the performing arts and music, with their frequent focus on voices and bodies, are central to these processes. **One perspective on gender is to observe the performative making of gender roles.** Virtually every performance reported in *Excursions in World Music* has something to do with the performance of gender.

In her seminal work *The Second Sex* (1953), Simone de Beauvoir wrote that the concept of woman is typically designed to be purposefully vague, because it needs to be able to change to accommodate the changeable concept of "man," which is similarly vague and which it is designed and redesigned to help define by contrast. The exigencies of history, in other words, require different (male) subjects, and that means that as the gender "man" changes to suit circumstances, "woman" transforms as well. This changeability and ambiguity assure that there are any number of concepts of men and women under construction, maintenance, and revision at any one time in a musical culture. To take "woman" as an example: there are good wives and mothers whom men must protect; wild women who have broken men's hearts, or whom men must tame; fallen women who represent to us the tragedies of life; objects of desire whom men pursue, often in vain, thus confirming the ideality of love in its unrequitedness.

These "many faces of woman" may seem like just more and more ways that real women are backed into corners and deprived of real chances at subjectivity, and indeed that is part of de Beauvoir's argument. But the necessity of performing these roles puts real women in places of real power, however constrained; and the inherent ambiguity of the roles themselves is a source of power as well, indicating as it does a latitude of which women can take advantage.

The origins of the Algerian popular music called *raï* provide one example. In the first decades of the 20th century, *shaykha* female singers who entertained in cabarets and other venues in the port city of Oran "were both singers and dancers who used their voices and bodies to crystalize desire in their male audiences" (see *Excursions*, Chapter 3). This forum, based in the power of seduction, enabled Shaykha Remitti, the "mother of raï," to sing of current political issues, migration, religion, and the sufferings of the marginalized, and to found an entire genre which would take North Africa and parts of Europe by storm as a form of social critique. The nightlife culture became a space outside of the everyday where extraordinary things could happen, including the construction of new gendered persons. Shaykha took stage names to protect their families, and reinvented themselves as a new kind of woman with a new kind of voice. They became symbols of modernity as women defying traditional gender prohibitions, and invented raï as a genre of social critique, pathos, and entertainment, and a "voice of modernity" (see Weintraub and Barendregt 2017 for many other examples of this phenomenon worldwide).

The gender "under construction" in the early history of raï is thus a complex one, a new, modern woman, with a new social power, preoccupied with a struggle for respectability. The struggle was particularly intense because the shaykha were women of high social power but low social prestige, historically associated with brothels and prostitution. They were one of many different kinds of performer who demonstrate the deep connections between entertainment and sexual labor, between musical expression and amorous play, between art, exploitation, and power.

With the liberation of Algeria from France in 1962 the new government clamped down on the entertainment culture in which the shaykha thrived, and while it continued as an alternative space of culture, men became the new standard bearers of the emergent genre. Women still frequented the nightlife spaces of raï, but as patrons, not singers. Women could still be found singing the risqué songs of raï at weddings, a rather more respectable setting that allowed them to shake former associations with sex work and that, at least seemingly, put the music in service of conventional social reproduction. The cabaret scene remained a space beyond everyday conventions, however, and now became a forum for men to diverge from conventional forms of masculinity and "display indeterminate markers of sexual identity" (Schade-Poulsen 1999: 141). These transgressions, however, were often accompanied at the cabaret by compensating gestures of hyper-masculinity, often resulting in violent brawls between singers and patrons (ibid.: 142). One can also see this in much global heavy metal musical culture, which often sees machismo and violence performed in direct proportion to the amount of transgendering in play. Such relative freedom to display non-normative sexual and gender identities was extended to the atmosphere of wedding performance as well, but no counterbalancing display of normative sexualities was required.

We have not yet spoken directly of sexuality, or relations and identities based in sexual desire. Gender is not always defined with reference to sexuality; for instance, one can be asexual but have a clearly articulated gender identity. But in the above example the two are rather inextricably intertwined. **If genders are social positions, sexuality is one of the most important relations that links them**; and it coalesces into *sexual identities* which may fortify or destabilize genders. In any case, musical and other performances of gender, like those in raï described above and in the textbook, are often accomplished through presentations of desire,

13

which are often proclamations of sexual identity as well. Sexual identities seem to be less constructed than discovered and experienced by each of us; but like everything else, they are processual, worked out in performance, and articulated and coded using pre-existing or emergent systems of signification. We can see these processes of articulation in the case of the non-normative sexualities struggling to define themselves in and around raï.

Gender, Sexuality, and the Voice

Turning away from North Africa, we find a very different story of gender construction told by the rise of Bollywood film music over the course of the twentieth century in India—one that centers, in part, around **the voice**. As female performers sought new modes of respectability that would enable public performance and participation in public life, they turned away from the full-throated voices of traditional female singers, many of whom had been courtesans themselves and like the shaykha associated with sexual labor. A new, "high-pitched, nasal-sounding female voice" became conventional; a deferential, hyperfeminine voice suited to the "good-wife-and-motherly" ideals of the emergent middle classes. The voice was associated in particular with two sisters, Lata Mangeshkar and Asha Bhosle, who together recorded many thousands of songs for film playback (see *Excursions*, Chapter 2). At the same time, a gentle, boy-next-door voice became conventional for male singers, similar to the "civil voice" which Martin Stokes describes arising in the history of Turkish popular music at much the same time (2010: 77), one which also bore the unmistakable signs of the intimacy of new cardioid microphone technology, which enabled this kind of vocal intimacy on record and in live performance. These new voices became, through popular circulation, the mechanism by which gendered voices in India, Turkey, and elsewhere were radically reformed. There are similar stories to be told in North America about the rise of crooners in popular music and the transformation of male and female voices. All of these, taking genders and their right relations as the foundation, were means of creating new notions of what it meant to be Indian, Turkish, American, both ethnically and in terms of civic participation; and they were part of the means by which emergent middle classes consolidated power.

Gender, Sexuality, and Power

The nuances of gender and sexuality in performance are often centrally about power. Unsurprisingly the cultures of domination which sprang up under colonialism, which has impacted all of the worlds of music discussed in *Excursions*, often centrally involved tropes and practices of gender and sexuality. A main thrust of the "orientalist" imagination (see Said 1979) of the British in South Asia and the Middle East, the Japanese throughout East and Southeast Asia, and other imperial powers has framed colonial subjects and entire territories, as female, and in need of male imperial tutelage or stewardship. Subaltern performers have often been made to fulfill these Orientalist fantasies in performance, and have inadvertently helped in their creation. And in the wake of such colonial cultures, post-colonial nation states have often undergone rather explicit processes of "masculinization," meant to undo the supposed feminization of culture which is cast as either an enforced effect of colonialism or purportedly one of the reasons why the country was colonized in the first place. One example is the effort to "remasculinize" Korean epic story-singing (*pansori*) (see *Excursions*, Chapter 5).

In contrast with colonial "feminizations" of culture and people, colonial and neo-colonial stereotypes of "Africa," described in the "Music of Sub-Saharan Africa" chapter of *Excursions*, are often informed by notions of African men, in particular, as hyper-masculine to the point of "savagery." Thus "Africa" is portrayed as in need of the stewardship of a domesticated, Western masculinity at the level of the colonial state; and African women, in particular, are painted as helpless, in need of rescuing from unspeakable violence by Western or other first-world elites (see Ndaliko 2016, Chapter 4). The reality on the ground is quite different, as the remarkable catalog of women's musical activism at the end of *Excursions*, Chapter 8 testifies, much of which has been notably more effective in combatting violence against women than the efforts of Western charitable concerns. But these stereotypes are very difficult to dislodge. They cling to the African diaspora wherever it goes; they are one reason why so many African-American boys and men are murdered by authorities and others every year. And despite the central roles of African-American men (and women) and other people of color in the development of American LGBTQ+ scenes—for instance in the Harlem Renaissance of the 1920s and '30s and the Greenwich gay scene of the 1960s—stereotypes of black men and their musics as "hyper-masculine straight" are still commodity #1 in North American popular culture. This is yet another example of social power without social prestige. The collisions of gender, sexuality, and race are classic examples of *intersection*: when different modes of social identity overlap in processes of privilege or oppression.

Alternatives

The musical performance of gender and sexuality has so much to do with power and domination that it might occasionally appear to have little to offer those who don't identify with normative genders or sexual identities. But we also find within culture many alternative spaces of performance that people have designed to allow them relative freedom of self and expression, although these scenes may be coopted by mainstreams and made into commodities for sale. The 1990s New York City gay dance culture which Buckland describes (2002), where men strove to be themselves free of social constraint in the rarified spaces of clubs and dancefloors, is but one species of a global phenomenon with many forms. Looking to traditional musics, many people of non-normative sexual identities and genders find their way into traditional performance roles. The vocation of musician, dancer, or performer is in many places traditionally considered an alternative social position already, and tends to recruit from amongst people who are already marginalized. Signing on to one of these vocations condemns people to high social power and low social prestige, and to a unique place which is at once central to and marginal within culture. There are kinds of participation, however, which do not involve this sort of full-time commitment, in which the rarified space of selfhood becomes a positive complement to the rest of life.

There are several instances of such alternative spaces in *Excursions*. Korea has rich traditions of homosexual and transgender cultural practice, often associated with the performing arts, and homosexuality was rather more permitted in Korea than the West until the neo-Confucian Joseon Dynasty (1392–1910). The strict social strictures of the Joseon Dynasty compelled elites to repress or conceal homosexual practice, but a well-known culture of male homosexuality flourished among lower-class *namsadang* itinerant performers from the late Joseon Dynasty into the twentieth century. Homosexuality was decriminalized in 1948, the year of the end of the US occupation of South Korea, long (55 years) before decriminalization was effective throughout the United States. Nonetheless, neo-Confucianist conservatism about gender and sexuality persists, and LGBTQ+ people struggle for acceptance, although, as elsewhere, much progress has been made.

Korean shamanism has long served as a space of relative acceptance of gendered and sexual difference. In shamanist performance, shamans dress as maidens, as shamans, as male warriors, and as a host of spirits—some male, some female, others non-specified in terms of gender. Shamans modulate their voices and behaviors as they are possessed by the various spirits as well. There is a tremendous fluidity in performance of gendered appearance, voice, and behavior, and this means that in performance shamans are at liberty to deviate from the genders associated with their assigned sex, and from the sexuality which is assumed to cling to it. This fluidity, part of the *liminal* character of ritual performance, has become part of the cultural space in which ritual practitioners live. Although most Korean spirit-descended shamans are female, there is a small minority of men who are drawn to shamanism as well. There is a small culture of gay male shamans in the ecstatic tradition; and there are many women who embrace the transgendering aspects of shamanism as identities in themselves. Same-sex relationships are not openly celebrated, but they are not uncommon. Some contemporary shamans have come forward as allies in support of LGBTQ+ rights.

We find a similar case in Myanmar's Taungbyone Nats Festival, an annual event held in honor of the spirit pantheon in which supplicants make offerings to different spirits, one of many such animist events throughout Southeast Asia, others of which are described in Chapter 7 of *Excursions*. The spirit–human connection is managed by spirit mediums called *nat kadaws*, a term often translated as "spirit wives." Since the 1980s, transgender gay men have entered the *nat kadaw* vocation, and the Festival has become a rare occasion where they are able to be public about their gendered and sexual identities. Not every culture values publicity the way Western liberal thought does, and equates it so closely with freedom; some queer theorists have criticized this attitude as derived from masculinist thinking about the nature of freedom as the phallic (or phallocentric, or phallogocentric (Derrida 1981)) domination of public space (see Sinnott 2013). Put slightly hyperbolically, whereas the Western liberal subject has to fly a banner proclaiming itself from a giant phallic symbol in the town square to be considered truly free, in other parts of the world privacy can be a measure or a site of freedom, and does not automatically equal or index repression. Publicity, privacy, and intimacy do not always configure or line up in such tidy ways anyway. The Taungbyone Festival is, by all accounts, an important annual event that helps consolidate the Burmese gay/transgender community; but understanding the significance of its publicity and of the public nature of its performances must be determined through careful research.

We have had only a few pages to consider the vast complexities of music as a gendered and sexual practice; there are many paths we could take from here. I end by listing some of the themes in this essay:

- The performative construction of gender
- Expressions of sexual identity in musical performance
- Musical performances of gender and sexuality vis-à-vis relations of power
- Body, movement, and dress in musical performance
- The voice as a medium of teaching and propagating gender and sexual ideology
- Musical constructions of normative gender roles and sexual identities
- Fluidity and change in music and in gendered/sexual practice
- The creation of musical spaces for alternative gendered and sexual practices and identities
- Intersections of gender, sexuality, race, and national identity under colonialism and in general.

Do be on the lookout for other intersections as well—with class, with age, ability, and other parameters of culture—as you work through the various themes of this reader and encounter the many musical practices in *Excursions*.

References

de Beauvoir, Simone. 1953. *The Second Sex*. New York: Knopf.

Buckland, Fiona. 2002. *Impossible Dance: Club Culture and Queer World-Making*. Middletown, CT: Wesleyan University Press.

Butler, Judith. 1988. "Performative Acts and Gender Constitution: An Essay in Phenomenology and Feminist Theory." *Theatre Journal* 40/4 (December): 519–531.

Derrida, Jacques. 1981. *Dissemination*. Chicago, IL: University of Chicago Press.

Ndaliko, Chérie Rivers. 2016. *Necessary Noise: Music, Film, and Charitable Imperialism in the East of Congo*. New York: Oxford University Press.

Said, Edward. 1979. *Orientalism*. New York: Vintage Books.

Schade-Poulsen, Marc. 1999. *Men and Popular Music in Algeria*. Austin, TX: University of Texas Press.

Sinnott, Megan. 2013. "Dormitories and Other Queer Spaces: An Anthropology of Space, Gender, and the Visibility of Female Homoeroticism in Thailand." *Feminist Studies* 39/2: 333–356.

Stokes, Martin. 2010. *The Republic of Love: Cultural Intimacy in Turkish Popular Music*. Chicago, IL: University of Chicago Press.

Weintraub, Andrew, and Bart Barendregt. 2017. *Vamping the Stage: Female Voices of Asian Modernities*. Honolulu: University of Hawaii Press.

3

MUSIC AND RITUAL

Richard Jankowsky

Scholars have long been fascinated by ritual. Rituals order calendrical and life cycle progressions (holidays, birthdays, graduations, weddings, funerals), connect individuals to larger social solidarities (festivals, parades, protests), and provide some of our most profound transcendental spiritual experiences (religious rites, trance healing ceremonies). They put into play highly charged cultural symbols evoking history, myth, kinship, politics, morality, spirituality, and belonging to act upon people's experience of cosmological, political, and personal power. It is important to note, however, that the concept of ritual is not a universal category of human action, but rather, an intellectual category devised to help us understand a range of those actions. Thus, there is no universally valid definition of ritual. However, just as all societies have sonic practices that approximate the English-language concept of "music," activities defined as "ritual" are present across the globe and have certain general family resemblances. Ritual, in the sense I'm using it, is an activity involving others that uses symbolic communication and performance to create an immersive experience deliberately located apart from the "everyday" world. It exercises the imagination to provide participants with a profound sense of what is possible. It is often teleological—that is, it moves toward a predictable goal—and therefore provides an experience of social synchrony through time. Ethnomusicological studies reveal that, when music is involved, ritual is not merely accompanied by music, but instead often serves as a showcase highlighting music's capacity to act on individuals and society.

Because some of the most influential studies of ritual focused on practices such as African initiation rites, Australian totemism, and Balinese ritual combat drama, ritual is sometimes associated with the "traditional" practices of "other" societies. However, ritual is prevalent, in many guises, in all societies, including twenty-first century North America, where people engage in ritual practices to pursue socially meaningful, personally transformative, heightened experiences of their world. As Joshua Pilzer argues in Chapter 5 of *Excursions*, even rituals that are anchored to a sense of a timeless past continue to speak to contemporary concerns and issues and are productively understood to be "resolutely modern." This chapter examines three domains of ritual experience as it relates to music: (1) trance healing rituals in which music is understood to facilitate encounters with unseen beings; (2) rituals of state and public spectacle in which music acts to provide a sense of solidarity that may reinforce (or challenge) political power; and (3) the ritualization of musical listening, whereby, for example, attending concerts can become a ritual act with outcomes similar to so-called traditional rituals.

Before moving on to our case studies, a few words on the transformational potential of ritual and the power of music are in order. While ritual commonly reworks social relationships, it is also individually transformative. Arnold van Gennep (2004 [1909]) proposed a three-part model of the experience of rites of passage involving (1) separation: the initiate is separated from the everyday world of society and enters the space of ritual; (2) liminality: in ritual, the initiate is in a deeply transformative yet ambiguous state of betweenness where they detach from their previous identity and gain new experiences and perspectives; and (3) reaggregation: the initiate returns to society transformed, with a new status in society. Van Gennep's model can be applied as much to healing rituals in which patients enter ill and leave healed as it can to the experience of college students going through the ritualized experiences of entering a specific place and finite period of higher learning before reincorporating into society at commencement with a new status of degree-holding graduate. Victor Turner's (1970) study of the ritual process zeroed in on the stage of liminality, finding in it a profound space of in-betweenness that also produces a sense of solidarity he called "communitas."

This sense of communitas has been linked to the role of music in ritual. In his study of a South African spirit possession ritual, John Blacking (1985) elaborated how music in such contexts is felt to be so powerful because it produces a strong sense of "fellow-feeling" for all participants, not only those who become pos- sessed by ancestor spirits. In his example, several types of participant take part in the ceremony: musicians and dancers of the local ritual community, members of neighboring ritual communities, non-member audience members who join in the performance, and spectators who do not perform. Blacking's holistic approach to ritual accounts for the transformative experience of all constituencies. He argues that, through the music, all those gathered have access to heightened experiences of the self and other, manifest in fellow-feeling (the social) and a transcendent sense of self (the individual). The work of music in ritual, then, is closely bound up with this interface between the self, others, and larger forces (political, social, and spiritual) and continually reinforces its own capacity to create the conditions for individuals to transcend their everyday selves.

Rituals of Healing and Trance

In many rituals of healing, music is used to create the conditions for individuals to enter into trance, a heightened or altered state of consciousness that some ritual communities cultivate to gain access to a domain of unseen beings. Gilbert Rouget's (1980) monumental study of music and trance concluded that there are no specific rhythms, melodies, instrumentation, or other musical features that automatically cause trance in listeners. Rather, trancers are culturally conditioned to respond to musics associated with trance in their own societies; as such, trance musics in one culture tend to differ substantially from trance musics in other cultures. Music tends to be necessary for eliciting trance states, yet there are no musical universals for doing so. This is one of many paradoxes of trance and music that also include the performance of private suffering in public settings and the high degree of self-control that is necessary for entering a state in which trancers give up control of the self. Another is in the realm of temporality: while trance rituals often mark the passage of time, they also have their own internal temporality, built on an "architecture of time" (Rouget 1986) provided by music. Spirit possession and shamanism are two cases in point.

Spirit possession and shamanism are two broad categories of ritual that involve healing and rely on music for efficacy. In spirit possession, an individual is understood to be temporarily inhabited, ridden, or displaced by possessing spirits, while shamanism often operates in the opposite fashion, with the shaman's soul understood to depart the body for a journey into the world of spirits (although shamans can also be possessed by spirits). The more categorical difference, however, is that in spirit possession, the patient in need of healing is the one who is inhabited by the spirit; the patient's trance dance is central to her own healing process. By contrast, in shamanism the shaman heals others. Chapter 3 in *Excursions* described a spirit possession ceremony in North Africa, where spirits from sub-Saharan Africa are summoned through musical sounds and instruments associated with the history of sub-Saharan migrations into North Africa.

Like similar rituals performed in Morocco and Algeria, the Tunisian stambeli ceremony involves the invocation of dozens of spirits (and several Muslim saints). Because each spirit has his or her own song, the musical repertoire is as large as the pantheon of spirits. Music is absolutely necessary to summon the spirits; without it, there can be no ceremony, and no healing. The purpose of the music is to attract the spirit, who will descend into ritual once he or she hears their song, which not only praises the spirit but also must be played skillfully to entice the spirit. In fact, if patients fail to fall into trance, a different (usually older, more experienced) set of musicians may be hired to try to correct the problem. Musical aptitude, then, is particularly important in spirit possession ceremonies, and ritual efficacy is largely in the hands of musicians. A successful trance experience entails the spirit accepting the invitation to descend into ritual, where it inhabits the body of the dancing host (the patient), until the spirit has had its fill of this rare opportunity to experience the power of the human world through music and dance.

A stambeli ritual depends on the effective deployment of the distinctive sounds of its bass-register lute (*gumbrī*) and iron clappers (*shqāshiq*), both of which index a sub-Saharan otherness that is at once associated with stambeli's power to deal with African spirits and its history of social marginalization. Beyond the sounds themselves, the ritual is structured according to a "chain" (*silsila*) of songs that brings each spirit to the ritual space in a loosely prescribed order. Each of these songs relies on a short, cyclic rhythmic ostinato that provides a cushion of reliably predictable movement through time. These rhythms increase in speed as the dancer's trance increases in intensity (compare the beginning and ending tempo of the listening example "Sīdī Marzūg" in *Excursions*, Chapter 3). Ritual time and efficacy relies on the aesthetic forces of music at the macrolevel (structuring of the ceremony) and the microlevel (creating the conditions for the trajectory of each trance dance).

Musical performance is equally important to shamanism (see *Excursions*, Chapter 5). In Korea, where two forms of shamanism are practiced, the music comes from the wellspring of traditional Korean music—unlike the migrational history of stambeli. In ecstatic shamanism, in the central and northwest regions of Korea, the shaman is possessed by spirits who then offer advice to and help the shaman manage the patient's afflictions caused by imbalances in the spirit world. In hereditary shamanism, limited to the southwestern part of the peninsula, shamans play more of a priestly role, serving as a mediator between humans and spirits in a less embodied way in rituals that are now declining in demand, albeit still active particularly in funeral rites. Music in ecstatic shamanism, based on the *janggo* hourglass drum and other drums and gongs, supports every stage of the ceremony, from opening instrumental pieces and the shaman's chants invoking the spirit to the dance performed by the shaman as she becomes possessed. More music proceeds as the spirit demands various forms of entertainment, and there is also a closing chant and dance to send off the spirit. But this description does not do justice to the way that music transforms the ritual sense of time through shifts between patterns, increases in tempo, and sudden endings. The ritual journey of the shamanic ceremony may oscillate between metered rhythmic patterns and free rhythmic sections. A free rhythmic section may gradually become regular, accelerating and turning into a rhythmic pattern (such as *jandgan*), effectively creating order, regularity, and intensity out of the flowing nature of the free rhythm passages.

The sounds of trance rituals situate participants in a space where notions of time and space are collapsed. Spirits representing neighboring societies and different historical eras are brought together in the same ritual, evoking social and political transformations. In Tunisia, timeless spirits from sub-Saharan Africa migrated along with stambeli's originators, sharing space with spirits representing nineteenth-century Ottoman rulers and Muslim saints from the thirteenth to the twentieth centuries. Political leaders sought out stambeli publicly, for example in performances for the Ottoman court in the nineteenth century, and privately, as members of the president's family sought out the healing services of stambeli ritual in the twenty-first century. In Korea, shamanism responds to national tragedies such as the financial crisis of 1997, the suicide of the former president in 2009, and a tragic ferry sinking in 2014. Shamanism and spirit possession, then, react to and absorb worldly, political powers. And the opposite is true: such political powers have also relied on the power of ritual, as the next section illustrates.

Rituals of State and Public Spectacle

Public rituals of state also enlist music in invoking powers, but those powers are worldly, political ones (although some may be understood to derive their power from the unseen realm of divinities). In our global geography, defined by borders between countries, each nation-state depends on bringing together three elements: a bounded geographic territory, a ruling apparatus, and the idea of a unified "people." Certain musical systems are used to legitimize political power through ritual musical performance. Asian court musics, for example, performed in ceremonies at royal courts and temples, signify prestige and authority, and governments have lavished resources on them to maintain their vitality. A Confucian philosopher once noted that giving verbal commands is less effective than enacting rituals because verbal commands always carry with them the possibility that the subject will consider doing the opposite. Rituals are more effective because they have no opposite (Turino 2008: 195).

The Maritime Southeast Asia chapter in *Excursions* (see Chapter 7) describes the importance of orchestral gong music to political authority across the region, focusing especially on the Indonesian states of Bali and Java. In Java, elaborate and expensive bronze gamelan orchestras are given proper names and offerings are made to them; the largest gongs can take a month to build. The instruments of the gamelan orchestra were ritual objects invested with power, not only because of the high value of bronze, but also because the highly ritualized forging process combines elemental substances (metal) and elemental forces (fire) associated with the supernatural (Spiller 2008: 47). The elaborate gamelan orchestras of the courts were not only symbols of wealth and prestige but also symbolized the legitimacy and power of rulers. Gamelan performances were central aspects of public ceremonies that demonstrated the potency of political authority by attracting followers and competing with the followings and ceremonies of neighboring leaders (Errington 1989: 286).

But there is much more to the ritual power of gamelan. First, the structure of the music is understood to represent the structure of the universe, with a cyclic ordering of time interpreted as mirroring the progress of time and space, thus embodying the cosmic order (Spiller 2008: 70). Second, gamelan's musical stratification mimics Javanese social stratification: in both cases, each musical part or social class has its place in the social hierarchy and must fulfill its "designated role" in "maintaining the status quo" (Spiller 2008: 70). According to Henry Spiller, by "regarding the exaggerated musical stratification in gamelan music as beautiful, listeners are predisposed to accept social stratification as the natural order of things," and gamelan music thus participates in normalizing people's acceptance of limited access to that power and prestige (Spiller 2008: 70). After Indonesian independence, court styles became redefined as national heritage, and new arts academies and performance contexts emerged that nevertheless maintain the chains of value connecting contemporary performance with the prestige and power of ancient Javanese courts. One gamelan piece associated with the courts that is still performed in many different gamelan settings is "Puspawarna," which announces the arrival of the prince (see Listening Guide in *Excursions*, Chapter 7). Listen to how different instruments play at different rates of speed to create a hierarchical layering whereby the largest instruments are struck less frequently than small instruments; the largest gong, which orients the timeline of the piece, is struck every 16 beats.

Gagaku in Japan illustrates the role of music in sonically legitimizing national authority. Gagaku was the music and dance of the Japanese imperial court as far back as the eighth century, when it established the Gagaku Institute to train court musicians. Featuring a solo voice and a small heterophonic instrumental ensemble, it is associated with refinement and elegance; the term gagaku, which translates to "virtuous," connects music to highly regarded social values. Over the centuries, gagaku remained associated with imperial power, even when the imperial system was replaced by the shogun system (1603–1868). When the Meiji empire reintroduced the position of emperor in 1868, it looked to gagaku as a tool to legitimize its rule. Gagaku served as a tool for cementing the new imperial system, legitimizing the lineage back to mythological origin of country, which made gagaku a tool of nationalists starting in the 1930s. When it was performed at the court, in Buddhist temples, and now on stage, the otherworldly timbres and elastic rhythmic forms of gagaku pieces like "Etenraku" (see *Excursions*, Chapter 6) reflect and further entrench its sacred and royal associations and its symbolism of the Japanese nation. Gagaku now plays a role in sonically invoking the political foundations of Japanese heritage.

Music is commonly mobilized in national anthems, parades (see the junkanoo example in *Excursions*, Chapter 11, for instance), and other civic activities designed to promote the idea—and feeling—not only of a unified nation, but also that the nation is the natural and primordial unit of belonging and loyalty. Indeed, ritual, broadly speaking, is an exercise of power, to make "a power situation appear a fact in the nature of the world" (Bloch 1989: 45). When fans in a baseball stadium rise, remove their caps, and sing along (or mouth the words) to the Star-Spangled Banner before a game, or "God Bless America" during the seventh-inning stretch, this is an act of what Benedict Anderson calls "unisonance": the sonic production and "echoed physical realization of the 'imagined community' of the nation-state" (2006: 145).

Yet because it defies the strict notions of ownership that nationalism depends on, music can also create spaces for alternative perspectives. National anthems are a case in point. While nationalism is exclusionary and rigid—demanding loyalty on its own terms—musical performance may reveal fissures in nationalist agendas and open up opportunities for resistance. When Jimi Hendrix performed the Star-Spangled Banner in a heavily distorted, feedback-laden electric guitar solo at Woodstock, he reclaimed the anthem for African Americans and a new generation opposed to war and dedicated to the Civil Rights Movement. Similarly, when Matoub Lounes sang the Algerian national anthem in Berber—the language of the country's indigenous population

24

excluded from Algeria's Arabic-based nationalist project—he helped bolster the Berber rights movement (see *Excursions*, Chapter 3). When Canadian students sang their national anthem on the occasion of the British Queen's royal visit, they did so by singing the anthem not only in Canada's official languages of French and English, but also in the indigenous languages of Cree and Inuktitut, emphasizing the limits of official national symbols in representing the mosaic of peoples who make up Canada's citizenry (see *Excursions*, Chapter 13). In all these cases, the performance of national anthems provides a critique of existing assumptions about the nation and opens up possibilities for reimagining the nation.

Listening as Ritual

If ritual, as the above examples suggest, is often deeply musicalized, the act of listening to music can also be ritualized. Some cultures put a name on the transformative, emotionally charged individual listening experience. In the Arab world, that experience is called ṭarab, a heightened state of emotion often described as a kind of musical ecstasy resulting from deep, attentive listening to music. In contrast to what is referred to as the "high arousal" trance state of spirit possession and shamanism, ṭarab may be interpreted as a "low arousal" trance state in which listeners may be emotionally transformed and respond physically at musically appropriate moments with silence and stillness, verbal exclamations, hand-clapping, or weeping. Ṭarab relies on a "feedback loop" (Racy 1991) between performer and listener, in which the variations and improvisations of the performer move the listener to react physically or verbally, which further empowers the artist to continue a masterful performance, which again moves the listener, and so on. The ritualized framing of the concert event encourages participants to focus their attention on specific performative aspects, such as the nuances of timbre or melodic phrasing and improvisation in ṭarab culture. These elements are magnified in concert performance and draw attention to the aesthetic force of these inner elements and processes that carry listeners through their journey, transform their emotional states, and generate meaning. Indeed, the song "Ghannīlī Shwayya Shwayya" (see *Excursions*, Chapter 3) not only evokes ṭarab (which you can hear in audience responses), but is also about the experience of ṭarab, drawing attention to the power of music to move us. Such experiences are associated with live performances, both public and private. Just as other rituals are structured in a predictable yet flexible way, so too do concerts have a ritualized structure with warmups, encores, climaxes, and the ebbs and flows of tension and release that audiences expect. But attending performances also pulls listeners into a larger whole. Performances are multisensory experiences, in which participants are not being told something but are made to experience something (Bell 1997: 160). The framing of the event creates a holistic totality apart from the everyday, holds at bay the chaos of quotidian life, and can present a microcosm of imagined or ideal social relations.

25

Classical music concerts in the United States, for example, are ritual occasions that celebrate "upper-middle-class and elite values and heritage and, for some concertgoers, are as much about the ritual occasion as about the music being performed" (Turino 2008: 61; Small 1987). Concertgoers take part in contemplative listening characterized by a deeply ritualized silence that honors "the taboo against talking, singing, dancing, and eating or drinking" (Kingsbury 1989: 165). Bruno Nettl (1995) interprets the classical music concert as a ritual event celebrating musical deities ("great composers") that is run by a priesthood (musicians, conductors, scholars) who interpret sacred texts (authenticated original versions of compositions) that are performed in ritualized settings (concerts) in architectural monuments that serve as shrines (concert halls, which often have the names of "deities" such as Beethoven and Bach inscribed on them). Indeed, as Andrea F. Bohlman notes in Chapter 9 of *Excursions*, the German city of Bayreuth is a site of pilgrimage for classical music aficionados to make the "once-in-a-lifetime journey" to:

> the concert hall built on top of a hill by the nineteenth-century German composer Richard Wagner just outside the city limits of this the southern German city. The building was designed for the purpose of performing Wagner's compositions, especially the four-evening cycle of operas he composed based on the German epic, *The Ring of the Nibelungen* (1848–74). Little luxuries build up the sensory delight: at the intermission people order sausages, pretzels, and sparkling wine.
>
> (Chapter 9)

Unlike some religious pilgrimages in which pilgrims "musically perform their spiritual journeys into existence" (Bohlman 1997: 80), these musical pilgrimages treat music with religious-like reverence. The ritual of pilgrimage often involves an arduous physical journey or, in some cases, the taxing tedium of air or rail travel; in either case the destination is a highly valued site of ritual activity. These destinations evoke both belonging and otherness: pilgrims may travel alone or in small groups but find and join forces with others to form a collectivity of like-minded participants. At performances held at musical pilgrimage sites, temporary microworlds are created by the atomized collectivity. Pilgrimages to dance clubs and electronic dance music (EDM) festivals on the circuit of techno-tourism in Europe, for example, are also undertaken in the pursuit of profound, transcendental experiences of music (see *Excursions*, Chapter 9). Going to raves or clubbing and listening to EDM is particularly associated with ritualized, spiritual experiences. Rave culture has its own philosophies of spirituality and transcendence, often drawing on sacred symbols and concepts from religions such as Buddhism and Hinduism, with a DJ sometimes referred to as a "shaman" who leads dancers on their ritual journeys with music that, like possession ceremonies, transforms consciousness by creating compelling temporal and spatial worlds (Sylvan 2005). Electronic dance music, based on repetition and gradual transformations, carries listeners through a sonic and psychic journey of heightened experience. These associations remain embedded in the musical sounds even when they are recontextualized outside the ritualized live performance experience and packaged into recordings that allow for portable, solitary listening experiences.

Indeed, such solitary listening experiences can produce similar autonomic nervous system arousal as ritual, such as goosebumps, chills, and changes in heart rate and emotional states. In ritual, when we listen to music, we entrain to it, meaning we become in sync with it and therefore also with others, including not only musicians but also a community of other listeners. There is great power in this. Traces of this power are extended even to solitary listening practices. Even when we think our musical experience is solely individual (think of listening through earbuds as you go to class), it still carries with it the underlying foundations and associations of ritualized music with its twin pillars of belonging and otherness. Everyday listening often occurs in conjunction with individualized rituals like studying, exercising, getting pumped up for a game or exam, or just chilling out. Such acts of listening all draw on the power of music—highlighted in rituals such as those discussed in this chapter—to create an atmosphere that envelops us, to help us transcend our ordinary sense of self, and to evoke a sense of connection to others, both present and absent.

References

Anderson, Benedict. 2006. *Imagined Communities: Reflections on the Origin and Spread of Nationalism.* London and New York: Verso.

Bell, Catherine. 1997. *Ritual: Perspectives and Dimensions.* New York and London: Oxford University Press.

Blacking, John. 1985. "The Context of Venda Possession Music: Reflections on the Effectiveness of Symbols." *Yearbook for Traditional Music* 17: 64–87.

Bloch, Maurice. 1989. *Ritual, History and Power: Selected Papers in Anthropology.* London: Athlone Press.

Bohlman, Philip V. 1997. "World Musics and World Religions: Whose World?" In *Enchanting Powers: Music in the World's Religions*, edited by Lawrence E. Sullivan, 61–90. Cambridge, MA: Harvard University Press.

Errington, Shelly. 1989. *Meaning and Power in a Southeast Asian Realm.* Princeton, NJ: Princeton University Press.

Kingsbury, Henry. 1989. *Music, Talent, and Performance: A Conservatory Cultural System.* Philadelphia, PA: Temple University Press.

Nettl, Bruno. 1995. *Heartland Excursions: Ethnomusicological Reflections on Schools of Music.* Urbana, IL and Chicago, IL: University of Illinois Press.

Racy, Ali Jihad. 1991. "Creativity and Ambience: An Ecstatic Feedback Model from Arab Music." *The World of Music* 33/3: 7–28.

Rouget, Gilbert. 1986. *Music and Trance: A Theory of the Relations between Music and Possession.* Translated by Brunhilde Biebuyck. Chicago, IL: University of Chicago Press.

Small, Christopher. 1987. "Performance as Ritual: Sketch for an Enquiry into the True Nature of a Symphony Concert." In *Lost in Music: Culture, Style, and the Musical Event*, edited by A. Levine White, 6–32. New York: Routledge & Kegan Paul.

Spiller, Henry. 2008. *Focus: Gamelan Music of Indonesia.* 2nd edition. New York and London: Routledge.

Sylvan, Robin. 2005. *Trance Formation: The Spiritual and Religious Dimensions of Global Rave Culture.* London: Routledge.

Turino, Thomas. 2008. *Music as Social Life: The Politics of Participation.* Chicago, IL: University of Chicago Press.

Turner, Victor. 1970. *The Ritual Process.* London: Routledge & Paul.

van Gennep, Arnold. 2004 [1909]. *The Rites of Passage.* London: Routledge.

4

COLONIALITY AND "WORLD MUSIC"

Chérie Rivers Ndaliko

In addition to offering insights into musical genres, instruments, artists, and practices, *Excursions in World Music* also provides an opportunity to explore the history of power. Its chapters invite us to explore many places, and, if we are paying attention, they also give rise to critical questions about how we understand and study the world—about how it has been divided into territories, what those territories are called (and who gets to decide), about who occupies them and on what terms they do so.

These are all questions about space, time, and power. And they are deeply embedded in *Excursions*. If, rather than approaching this text (primarily) as a study of music and sound, we approach it as a study of space, we might ask ourselves, for example, why the book divides the world into the regions it does? Which places are included? Which, if any, are left out? Which places get greater or lesser attention? Why are there three chapters dedicated to East Asia (China, Korea, and Japan) and one chapter for all of Sub-Saharan Africa? For that matter, why is Sub-Saharan Africa separated from North Africa? Why do European languages determine what we learn about Central and South America—that is, why do we learn about Spanish and Portuguese speaking areas of Latin America and not Dutch, French, and English territories? Better yet, why are Nahuatl, Quechua, or Guarani not the languages around which the study of Central and South America is organized? (And why is that region of the world called "Latin America" anyway?).

I raise these questions not to critique the choices made by the editors and authors of *Excursions* but rather to provoke reflection on how we conceive of the world. Many people have been conditioned not to question, in depth, the boundaries and systems that make up the modern world, but to regard them as the result of bygone history, as economic inevitabilities, or simply as geographic realities.

But from another perspective, the modern world is a testament to a very specific form of power called coloniality (also called the coloniality of power or the colonial matrix of power) that has come to dominate the globe.[1] We will arrive at a more detailed definition of coloniality, but in broad strokes it refers to a system of interrelated hierarchies—including racism, patriarchy, capitalism, heteronormativity, Western epistemology, neoliberalism, and others—that permits a dominant group to exercise power over subordinate groups with or without formal mechanisms of control. The issue of formal structures is critical—indeed the term coloniality arose out of the need to identify the persistence of Western domination and hegemony both preceding the establishment and following the dismantling of European and U.S. American colonial administrations.

A number of important characteristics differentiate coloniality from other forms of power. One is that coloniality rests on assumptions—about race, gender, governance, knowledge—which, though false, have been so thoroughly normalized that they are not only accepted as truths, but as foundations of reality (and the only possible version of reality at that). Therefore recognizing coloniality can be difficult—after all, it persists by disguising itself as "reality" or simply "how the world is." To learn to recognize coloniality we must, then, begin by investigating these entangled assumptions and how they have come to stand in for truth.

Manufacturing Race and Space

One primary axis on which coloniality operates—both historically and in the present—is race. To untangle the relationship between race and global power structures we must revisit a number of things that began in Western Europe, for though they happened more than five centuries ago, these events directly shape our understanding of the world today. The story of coloniality is rooted in the age of exploration, during which Europeans sought to expand their empires. Over a few centuries, they claimed new territories and conquered the peoples who inhabited them. This was a violent process involving the theft of land and the slaughter and enslavement of millions upon millions of human beings.

Clearly Europeans were not the first to covet foreign lands. There have been feuds between people throughout time, resulting in the domination of one group by another. What is unique about the era of European exploration—indeed about coloniality—is that it was not an effort to dominate one, or even a handful of neighboring groups, but rather to dominate the world. Justifications for this level of domination evolved over time. What began as religious conquest in the name of God, gave way to imperial conquest in the name of the state. Through this process, the modern notion of race was invented and used to explain Europeans' "right" to conquer and control others. In the Americas, race was first understood as phenotypic, then as biological; in Africa, biology was transferred to skin color. In all cases, the notion of race was used to justify imperial and colonial violence.

And this directly impacts our modern understanding of space. Indeed, European explorers and cartographers sought not only to map physical geography (e.g. lands and waters), but also to locate and classify different races of human beings. Their classifications identified Europeans as the superior race, seconded by Asians, whose culture and "civilization" could not be denied, and, on the bottom of this hierarchy were indigenous peoples of the Americas and antipodes, as well as black Africans. Over time, systems of racial classification added categories for mixed race populations (e.g. *castizo, mestizo, cholo, mulato, indio,* and *zambo* as discussed in *Excursions,* Chapter 10) determined by their percentage of "whiteness." The classification of races was accepted as cutting edge science, which had severe consequences. Claiming racial hierarchy as scientific fact implied that it was objective and incontestable truth—that is, that European racial superiority was not a human invention but a scientific law of nature.

In truth, codifying the difference between conquerors and conquered as biological was a means of reconciling violent domination with Christian notions of morality. Inventing race, in effect, transferred the justification of conquest from greed to "science," enabling "white" Europeans to dominate lands and peoples around the world in the name of "moral duty." Exercising such domination required strategic laws to protect the rights and properties of white people while still permitting the conquest of the "New World." To achieve this, a 1559 treaty between France and Spain designated, as "amity lines," the prime meridian and the tropic of cancer. To the north and west of these amity lines the rule of law applied; to the south and east of them it did not. Notably, this treaty applied to people and property not *in* but *from* territories north and west of the amity lines. Thus white people and their goods were (and arguably still are) afforded legal protections when they were in, say, Africa, while black Africans were (and arguably are) not afforded the same in Europe.

It was thus disguised as science and law that race and the idea of racial hierarchy was naturalized as a "fact" rather than a very subjective Eurocentric fiction. Of course racial "science" has long been debunked, but this history continues to influence how we learn about the world. To return to the opening questions of this chapter, this history explains why studies of global history (and world music), frequently examine East Asian nations thoroughly and as individual countries, whereas places lower on the racial hierarchy are grouped as generalizable regions. Similarly, it explains why North Africa, which is on the European side of the amity lines, is included with the Middle East and not with the rest of the continent, which is south and east of the lines. (It also explains why Egyptian civilization is typically taught as if it were not part of Africa.) In other words, the racialized cartographic activities of 15th century Europe continue to shape how we understand and study the world. To understand this is to begin to recognize coloniality.

From Race and Space to Capitalism

Though racial hierarchy is one primary ingredient, race alone does not sustain the colonial matrix of power. It is, rather, one in an entangled system of hierarchies. Capitalism is another. But from the perspective of coloniality studies, capitalism is not simply an economic system, but is, instead, constituted by racial (and other) hierarchies. This view of capitalism lays bare the inherent connections between race and global economic structures. Indeed, the very premise of capitalism—the production of surplus—relies on the exploitation of labor performed by people deemed "disposable" (in one way or another) by dominant groups. Historically, these were indigenous populations who Europeans placed on the bottom of the hierarchy of races, and to whom they assigned subhuman status in order to justify exploiting them as slaves and unwaged laborers. From this perspective, examples of musical hybridity and migration in Latin America and the Caribbean (discussed in Chapters 10 and 11 of *Excursions*) as well as in the United States (discussed in Chapter 13) are sonic echoes of coloniality for they are premised on the forced migration—historic and ongoing—of labor forces and the cultural practices they retain as they move through space. In cumbia, for instance, we quite literally hear what happened when bodies, transported and dominated for capitalist purposes, collided in coastal Colombia. As Chapter 10 describes, it resulted in an amalgam of musical practices drawn from Africans, Amerindians, and Europeans. The very makeup of cumbia ensembles, which includes, among others, hand drums and other percussion instruments associated with Africa, "indigenous" flutes associated with Amerindian traditions, and "Western" instruments like accordion, guitar, and bass, bears witness to the history of proximity forced through colonialism.

But, having colonial roots does not make cumbia an example of coloniality. Quite the contrary, like so many other hybrid musical forms, cumbia artists have transformed the genre, which was historically viewed as "low brow" by racial elites, into an emblem of identity and pride. What's more, some artists use such hybrid genres with colonial roots to make concertedly anti- or decolonial critiques that expose and/or reject coloniality (I will return to decoloniality in both concept and practice below). It is, however, important to recognize the influence of capitalism in this as well. Indeed, just as capitalism was the driving force behind the historic migrations that landed Africans and Amerindians in coastal Colombia, so, too, capitalism is the driving force behind the contemporary urban migrations that continue to shape the genre. I point this out not to diminish the impact of sounds like cumbia, but rather to underscore the interconnected elements of capitalism.

Viewing capitalism through the lens of coloniality also opens up other ideas related to music and culture. From this vantage point, capitalism is "an integrated network of economic, political and cultural processes the sum of which hold the system together."[2] Unlike other schools of thought that view the capitalist world system as primarily constituted *either* by culture (e.g. postcolonial theory) *or* by economic relations (e.g. political-economy theory), studying coloniality makes clear that the capitalist world system is constituted, fundamentally and equally, by both. And not just culture and economics, but also race, gender, sexuality, epistemology, and so on.

From this perspective, the discussion of how Europe influences other places becomes both an economic *and* a cultural question at the same time. And one that thus puts into perspective less tangible aspects of Western expansion and domination, including the notion of cultural and mental colonization. Indeed, by creating, in their colonies, dependence on European metropoles, colonizing nations did not just "underdevelop" their colonies in economic and political terms, they also promoted Western cultural superiority in ways that led many colonized populations to emulate the West in expressive and intellectual practices.

In short, culture, too, was—and is—a tool of coloniality. This was certainly true in Europe's African and Asian colonies, and of course this has sonic implications. As discussed in Chapter 5 of *Excursions*, the influence of military marching bands, Christian hymns, Western popular music, and Western classical music education, for example, significantly shapes the sonic landscape of Korea. There are, of course, countless examples, including *chindon-ya*, a type of distinctly Japanese street advertisement band combining both Japanese and Western influences (see *Excursions*, Chapter 6).

It is also important to point out that Europe was not the only colonizing force. To be sure, Europe set the example and the precedent, but other nations also exercised colonial power and coloniality. To cite a few examples: beginning in 1895, Japan colonized much of the Western Pacific and East Asia, including Taiwan, Korea, and China; the United States (itself already a settler colony), colonized, and/or established as "protectorates," parts of the Caribbean. These forms of colonization, too, are part of the larger picture of global coloniality and thus they, too, have sonic implications that are audible in *Excursions*. Indeed the larger point is, if we train our ears to coloniality, we hear in all these sounds potent reminders of the fundamental interconnections between culture, race, and capitalism.

From Race, Space, and Capitalism to Universal Truth

In addition to racial hierarchies and capitalism, another factor that sustains the colonial matrix of power is control over knowledge. This is relevant to the study of world music in that diverse methods of understanding the world have, over time, been disguised as absolute—and singular—truth. Indeed, from within the colonial matrix of power, there is only one legitimate way to understand the world and that is through modern Western science. Historically, this view is linked to a shift in European philosophy from conceptualizing knowledge as something divine (i.e. determined by God and interpreted by theologians) to something human, that is, objectively knowable by man (and I use the gendered pronoun to reflect the era).[3] This line of thought suggests there is a universal Truth that can be discerned by studying the laws of the material universe, which, is, of course, the foundational belief driving modern Western science and affirmed by modern Western theory.

Because it is framed as unveiling empirical Truth, modern Western science (aided by modern Western theory) claims total objectivity. By extension, everything undertaken in the name of modern Western science—whether natural, social, or political science—is deemed rational, accurate, and valid. And, critically, because it is deemed rational and accurate, what is undertaken in the name of modern Western science is deemed valid for *everyone everywhere*. This has a number of implications. For one, it justifies global political projects. For example,

33

economists promote development discourse in the name of science, political scientists promote democratization discourse in the name of science, natural scientists promote conservation discourse in the name of science. Without disputing the specific merits or shortcomings of any of these discourses, from the perspective of coloniality studies they all provide recipes with which to remake the rest of the world in the image of the West. For the imperative to "develop" is really to develop like the West; the imperative to adopt democracy is really to adopt neoliberal Western democracy; the imperative to conserve natural resources is really to apply the capitalist logic of management and control; etc. And, like the racial justifications behind imperial and colonial conquest, the continued imposition of Western ways of life is framed as "science."

A byproduct of viewing modern Western science as objective and thus universally true is that, from this perspective, no other form of knowledge can also be true. Thus in the name of modern Western science, all other ways of life are either deemed false, framed as folkloric or superstitious, destroyed, or some combination of the three. There is much to say about the destruction and falsification of non-Western epistemologies, but most relevant to this study of world music is, arguably, their designation as folklore and culture. Indeed, the colonial matrix of power persists, in part, by subsuming diverse cultural practices and, in so doing, stripping them of any real power. This happens through a number of subtle maneuvers in the way knowledge is institutionalized in the West. For example, labeling non-Western ideas under the umbrella of "culture" rather than "science" already separates them from (and implies they are not relevant to) economics, politics, and other privileged "scientific" forms of knowledge that inform geopolitical decisions.

Here, again, we encounter the artificial separation of culture from economics. And here, again scrutinizing the separation of culture from economics sheds light on the logic of coloniality. Indeed, in regards to capitalism, separating culture from economics obfuscates the complex and entwined forces sustaining the coloniality. In regards to epistemology, this division prevents us from taking seriously—even recognizing—any options other than those prescribed by the colonial matrix of power. For they have all already been deemed false by modern Western science. Thus they could not possibly prescribe a valid way of being. (This dynamic is, in part, what Didier Awadi challenges in "*Mon Afrique*" as discussed in *Excursions*, Chapter 8.)

This is how one view of the world makes itself universal: by eviscerating all others. In the colonial matrix of power, this involves labeling all non-Western forms of knowledge as "culture," which, under the hegemony of modern Western science is code for "not factual" and thus not True in any meaningful sense. (Notably, non-Western forms of knowledge do stand a chance of becoming "true" but only when validated by modern Western science—think acupuncture, yoga, Pachamama, etc.)

The "So What?" Factor

The manufacturing of race and its intricate interconnectedness with modern Western conceptions of space, capitalism, and knowledge are a few salient characteristics of coloniality. There are, of course, others, including the imposition of (Western) patriarchy and sexual norms; the "scientific" classification of humans as separate from "nature," which enables unchecked destruction of the environment. But what does all this mean for the study of world music? Investigating coloniality in the context of world music opens up an array of options. On one hand, it exposes some troubling insights into how—and why—modern Western institutions study other "cultures" as they do. Indeed, like anthropology, the field of ethnomusicology has been complicit in manufacturing and imposing racial hierarchies and in sustaining the perceived divide between culture and economics (as discussed in *Excursions*, Chapter 8). In these and other ways, the institutional study of world musics and world cultures has, ironically, diminished rather than increased their potential to provide viable alternative perspectives to the colonial matrix of power.

At the same time, recognizing music—and the study of music—as complicit in coloniality (hopefully) prevents further unconscious perpetuation of such complicity. Indeed learning to recognize coloniality opens possibilities for many pressing questions to emerge at the intersection of coloniality and sound. For example, what does, or could, music (and the study of music) do to make coloniality visible? or audible? How might we approach the study of music in ways that allow us to take non-Western practices and beliefs seriously without framing them as folkloric and/or denying their status as valid and true forms of (scientific) knowledge? And what might, or ought, studies of music contribute to decoloniality, that is, to creating options other than those prescribed by the colonial matrix of power?

Spurred by questions of this ilk, we can find in *Excursions* additional avenues through which to think about music and sound. For example, Chapter 8, "The Music of Sub-Saharan Africa," makes coloniality visible. By explicitly highlighting the ways music was instrumentalized in the invention of Africa, the chapter as a whole exposes the ongoing relationship between Western epistemology, Western economic interests, and the study of "African music." It also includes albums, such as Anjelique Kidjo's *Remain in Light*, that use lyrics, melodies, harmonies, and rhythms to expose capitalist violence and global hierarchies. Indeed the very fact that Kidjo, a Black Beninese woman, produced a remake of Talking Heads' iconic album draws explicit attention to issues of cultural appropriation—and coloniality—that often obscure African origins of popular global cultural practices.

In addition to making coloniality recognizable, *Excursions* also provides opportunities to take non-Western epistemologies seriously as conduits of knowledge. With this goal, one could pursue a range of compelling questions, for example, in the discussion of the spiritual and musical practice of *candomblé* in Brazil

(Chapter 10). While the chapter focuses primarily on the logistical and practical elements of candomblé, it includes clues one could pursue more deeply. Entering into trance, for instance, is often dismissed as "superstition" (by modern Western science), but from non-Western perspectives trance yields important factual information. In fact, the kinds of knowledge that keep human beings in balance with the natural environment are, in some cultures, linked to trance. In other cultures, such as Korea's shamanistic traditions (discussed in Chapter 5), the balance between humans and nature rests on the perception that all matter is infused with spirit, a view that is not dissimilar in principle, though distinct in practice, from the indigenous North American perspectives discussed in Chapter 12.

The point is, from these perspectives, learning to live in balance with nature would benefit Western societies. And, to return to candomblé, what of the combination of chickenblood, oil, and honey? Ought we to dismiss that as an exotic or primitive concoction or might we consider whether it has medicinal or other properties? The point here, is not to make a specific argument about a given practice (much less one I know little about), but rather to demonstrate the kind of curiosity that permits us to take non-Western epistemologies seriously as conduits of knowledge.

The final question to pursue is what studies of music might contribute to decoloniality. Before drawing examples from *Excursions*, it is important to outline, briefly, two key principles of decoloniality. First is that the decolonial school of thought adamantly rejects the idea that we are in a postcolonial world (and thus diverges from postcolonial thought). Indeed, the whole point of identifying coloniality is to name the matrix of power that persists despite the dismantling of formal colonial administrations.

A second important principle from the perspective of decoloniality is that antidotes to coloniality must be derived from options not predicated on the colonial matrix of power. The notion of options, here, is paramount. From a decolonial perspective, identifying any given option (e.g. matriarchy) exposes, by default, that dominant paradigms (e.g. patriarchy) are not in fact "reality" but rather they, too, are one in a menu of options. Thus taking or leaving them becomes a possibility (if not always a realistic immediate choice). From this perspective any form of resistance structured as "alternatives" (rather than "options") has already accepted, as primary, the power to which the alternative is necessary.

Recognizing that we still inhabit a colonial world and thinking in terms of options affords us greater freedom to identify—and choose—which options exist, which we might invent (or recover), and which to adopt. And this is one way music might contribute to decoloniality. There are, of course, individual songs and albums that explore options. Ancient Man's performance of "I Ain't Askin' Fa Much," for example, reminds listeners that returning to their roots (in his case African roots) can reconfigure identity in powerful ways (see *Excursions*, Chapter 11). In a similar vein, tracks on Anjelique Kidjo's *Remain in Light* point to Afrofuturism as a means by which to establish social and aesthetic ideals that are not rooted in colonial logic and racism. For example, to combat the racist association of whiteness with beauty that prompts many African women to bleach their skin (with severe health consequences), in "Seen and Not Seen" Kidjo asserts standards of beauty based on West African aesthetics (see *Excursions*, Chapter 8). In "Soul is Heavy," Nneka revives the memory of political activists fighting oil exploitation and environmental degradation in Nigeria (also Chapter 8).

Other songs and albums identify—and in some cases reclaim—more specific options. Didier Awadi's *Presidents d'Afrique* (discussed in *Excursions*, Chapter 8) is a good example. In it, he revives political speeches delivered by revolutionary African leaders, many of whom were assassinated and whose legacies have been either buried or distorted by coloniality. Reviving them quite literally presents an array of options to younger generations, who would not otherwise learn about the continent's most liberatory policies. (For example, in just three years as president of Burkina Faso, Thomas Sankara almost completely freed his country's economy from dependence on its former colonial power, France, while simultaneously increasing literacy rates from 13% to 73% and championing women's rights.)

But the decolonial options enacted through music go beyond individual songs and albums. The genre champeta, for example, is a testament to musical decoloniality. As indicated in Chapter 10 of *Excursions*, a primary feature of champeta is *Palenquero*, a creole that integrates Spanish with various Bantu languages spoken in Africa. But though the origins of Palenquero are colonial, the language is the result of centuries of decolonial activity. It developed in Palenque de San Basilio, a town established by escaped slaves in Northern Columbia that was freed by royal decree in 1691 (because they were helping too many Africans escape slavery) and thus the first free Black town in the Americas. Today, Palenquero is threatened by dominant languages like Spanish, thus singing in Palenquero is an active means of sustaining a long-standing decolonial tradition. In addition, by popularizing champeta, Black Colombians—who are marginalized in their country—transformed negative connotations about their identity into a source of pride and honor that is valued around the world.

Other links between music and decoloniality are measurable in economic terms. Take, for example, Malian singer Oumou Sangare (discussed in *Excursions*, Chapter 8), who leverages her stardom in projects—like building hotels and manufacturing affordable automobiles. Her music has enabled her to create economic options for local populations in Mali that do not rely on coloniality as exercised by neoliberal monetary bodies like the World Bank or the International Monetary Fund.

Then there are intersections between musical decoloniality and politics. Of this, the Senegalese Y'en a Marre and Burkinabé Balai Citoyen movements (also discussed in *Excursions*, Chapter 8) are a prime example. Founded by a group of rappers, journalists, and university students, these groups actively reintegrate "culture" and "economics" as they identify—and embody—options other than coloniality. Through music-driven grassroots social organizing, they have effectively reshaped West African political landscapes by galvanizing enough youth votes to oust corrupt presidents in both Senegal and Burkina Faso. In addition to large-scale political actions, they have also developed sustained opportunities for sociopolitical engagement that are not built on the colonial matrix of power but that, instead, support local communities in utilizing their resources—including non-Western forms of knowledge—to solve their own problems. In this way they support initiatives related to education, public health, economic development (as understood in local cosmologies), disaster relief and prevention, and much more. In sum, they have not only drawn inspiration, knowledge, and strategy from former leaders like Thomas Sankara and Patrice Lumumba, but adapted these historic efforts to the present.

The Take Away

Under the right circumstances, music can be a powerful means of exposing and embodying options not derived from the colonial matrix of power. So, too, the study of music can serve as an antidote to coloniality. But this requires discipline. It requires that we refuse to use "decoloniality" as a buzzword. That, instead, we discern, for example, between musical decoloniality and the popular—often general, sometimes apolitical, even vague—association of music with "resistance." There are, of course, monumental examples of musical resistance movements, including the Civil Rights and Anti-Apartheid movements (discussed in Chapter 8). These and other examples are important political actions undertaken through music. What recognizing coloniality adds is the capacity to see the multiple and entangled aspects of the dominant global system. And in this music can be a guide. If, that is, we guard against the dangers of claiming the "power" of music in abstract ways that risk relegating it to the domain of "culture" in a global system that divorces "culture" from "science."

And therein lies the challenge: to read books like *Excursions* without perpetuating coloniality, which is already embedded in the notion of "world music" (see the introduction to this Reader). To read *Excursions* decolonially is to read it not (primarily) as a study of music and sound, but as a roadmap of global power throughout time and space. That means constantly reading—and listening—against the grain by training your ears to what is omitted and sleuthing out why. It means unthinking and rethinking every assumption, expectation, and notion of "reality" or truth. It means taking other options seriously by adopting, as a mantra, the simple questions "according to who?" and "why?"

Notes

1 The terms "coloniality" and "coloniality of power" were first coined by Peruvian sociologist Aníbal Quijano. This chapter draws on the ideas of Quijano and many decolonial thinkers have subsequently built on his work including Walter Mignolo (who coined the phrase "the colonial matrix of power" and has done extensive work on the notion of

decolonial "options"), Sylvia Wynter, and Ramón Grosfoguel. My own thinking about decoloniality is also deeply influenced by Boaventura de Souza Santos.

2 Emmanuel Wallerstein. 1991. *Unthinking Social Science.* Cambridge: Polity Press. 230.

3 This idea is most commonly attributed to Réne Descartes (considered the founder of modern Western philosophy) and his famous phrase "I think/reflect therefore I am."

5

MUSIC AND SPACE

Marié Abe

Sound travels through space. Music is rooted in place. Sound helps orient us in space. Music can take you places. Sound can fill up space. Music recalls places you have been. Sound can get blocked from flowing into space. Music evokes places you have never been, or that don't even exist. Sound may disrupt existing spaces, or create new spaces. Whether you conceive of sound as vibrations in the air or as something to be perceived through your senses, sound is inextricably linked to space. Put another way, music and space are deeply entangled, almost inseparable.

The relationship between music and space is not merely about the acoustic physics—about how sound is created and propagated so that you hear and feel it in your body. Just as music is simultaneously an acoustic and social phenomenon that calls for cultural specificity in our critical listening, space, as you will see, also has as much to do with our thinking habits and ideas as it does with physical parameters. For instance, in our everyday speech, spatial metaphors abound. Perhaps you've used or heard expressions like, "try mapping out your ideas" or, "make space for more joy in your life," without giving them much conscious thought. But what do we mean by space, exactly? As we will see, we use several categories for thinking about space, and such everyday verbal expressions reflect only one of them—although a prevalent one, at that. Exploring these different categories of spatial thought raises so many questions about the nature and identity of space and its relation to music: is space necessarily a physically deline-ated unit, like a mappable territory, or is it a mental construct, like a home you have left behind, or a paradise? Is there a "space" that is beyond this physical and mental binary? Is space different from place? Does music give character to space, or does space assign character to music? Who gets to create, inhabit, or claim space through music over others? The spatial metaphors that we use in our everyday speech often suggest vision more than hearing; might *listening* to space conjure up a different understanding than *looking* at space? Must space exist before music can happen, or can music happen before space exists, creating a new space through its sounds?

This chapter explores how sound—musical or otherwise—compels us to think about, and through, space in different ways. In particular, I highlight how thinking about space inevitably leads to the issues of culture, power, and difference—difference conceived in the registers of race, ethnicity, nationality, class, sexuality, gender, age, etc. Such difference does not exist in the abstract, but is spatialized; a particular identity—and its sounds—can be attached to (or confined within, or excluded from) a neighborhood, region, country, diaspora, or even an imaginary place. Throughout *Excursions*, we encounter examples of how such spatialized differences are musically expressed, negotiated, produced, and contested. Music or sound can be a unifying expression of a national identity or a source of friction between neighboring communities of different ethnic heritages. Certain types of music may be used to stereotype the "Other" in a distant place. A marginalized immigrant community in a segregated neighborhood might uphold a song that captures their sense of belonging—a song that is rooted both in the memory of their homeland and their current location and serves as a symbol of resistance and pride. As a deeply entangled pair, then, space and music provides a particularly powerful way of examining the intersection of culture, power, and difference.

Below, I'll explore four different categories of spatial thinking and illustrate how sound and music can help us think about them by drawing on examples from *Excursions*: (1) "absolute space"; (2) "stirring up absolute space"; (3) "phenomenological space/soundscape"; and (4) "relational space." Within each conceptualization of space, we will pay close attention to the intersections of culture, power, and difference as we hear them playing out through a series of musical examples. You will see how each approach highlights different issues and themes: race, coloniality, nationalism, and stereotype (absolute space); migration and diaspora (stirring up absolute space); embodiment, class, and the everyday (phenomenological space/soundscape); and indigeneity, environment, and circulation (relational space). You might also find that, in some musical examples, more than one of these spatial conceptions may be present. Through these examples, I hope that you will come away with an expanded understanding of what space can mean, the important roles that music and sound play in these differently conceived notions of space, and the stakes and consequences of thinking through, and listening to, these different understandings of space.

1. Absolute Space: Space as Geographical Container

Nationalism and Coloniality

Consider, for a moment, what is happening when people play or sing their national anthems. These songs are intended to generate pride in one's membership in a "nation-state," a relatively new concept that is built on the assumption that political and cultural borders are or should be coterminous. According to this way of thinking, each stretch of space we call a country, geographically delineated and marked by physical borders, contains a particular national identity presumably shared among all its citizens, and symbolized by, among other things, the national anthem.

But cultural geographers Neil Smith and Cindi Katz have critiqued the underlying assumption being made here—namely that space is a pre-existing field, a passive container in which things happen. This understanding is called "absolute space." Smith and Katz (1993) show how this normalized notion, which many of us probably share, is rooted in the emergence of capitalist social relations in sixteenth-century Europe, which established absolute space as the premise that enabled the subsequent development of capitalism and colonialism. This idea that space is a surface (i.e. land) that is empty and inert, something one can partition and own, has led, on the one hand, to ideas about geographically delineated territories that contain unique national identities (nation-states), and, on the other, to colonial projects which (conveniently) conceived of land as a passive, commodifiable object, disregarding the lives and histories already contained therein.

Absolute space has been at the root of much of modern Western thought. For instance, it has shaped the "terrain" in which cultural difference is understood. In the absolutist conception of space, cultural difference is naturalized along geographical–cultural lines and immobilized as an historically, supposedly unchanging essence, thus painting a static picture of cultures as self-contained both in time and space. For example, for the proponents of a discourse positing Japan as a monoethnic nation (see *Excursions*, Chapter 6), a supposedly unique ethnic, religious, and cultural heritage is contained within the national boundaries. All area studies, as discussed in the introduction to this Reader, rest on this notion of absolute space; and academic disciplines growing out of such understandings of space study cultural difference as contained within geographical boundaries. Even the chapters of your textbook, *Excursions*, are organized on this principle.

From this perspective, music and space are often taken as a homologous pairing, in which the two echo and reinforce each other. Put another way, in absolute space, music is considered an innate expression of the distinct character of a given territory. For example, you might take a class (or read a chapter) on the "music of India" or the "music of the Middle East" and expect to learn about the internal coherence and overarching aesthetic similarities in the music of these geographical areas.

Race and Essentialist Stereotypes

These links to colonial projects and to assumptions about national coherence might suggest why a concept of absolute space can also be at the base of musical stereotyping. If space is an empty expanse to be owned, tamed, or ruled, then it can also be freely invested with ideas, sounds and images, regardless of the lived realities on the ground. This is the point at which representation and absolute space intersect. Musical sounds can be used to construct an entirely imaginary space and connect it to a real stretch of land. A good example of this is found in the discussion of musical representations of "Africa" in Western popular culture (see *Excursions*, Chapter 8). "Ooga booga" music in early Hollywood films produced and then normalized an idea of a space called "Africa" based on racist ideas that reduced the vastness, complexity, and dynamism of the entire continent into a singular narrative of a wild, uncivilized place inhabited by less-than-human people "stuck behind in time." The more recent *Lion King* example shows, again, how musical representations of "Africa" are stripped of the actual complexities, specificities, and humanity of the continent, turning it, for those who know Africa only through the film, into a monolithic, safari-like space inhabited by wild animals.

This might seem innocuous, except that the way we imagine spaces through representations has real-life, political consequences. Edward Said (Said 1978), who coined the concept "imaginative geography," calls our attention to how spatially confining the Other (in this example, people who live on the entire continent of Africa) in representational practice can be a means to domesticate and dominate the Other in very real colonial (and neo- or postcolonial) contexts. The colonization of Africa and the representational practices that, through musical stereotypes, render Africa as an absolute space (in one way or another devoid of culture and society), mutually reinforce each other.

"Absolute space," then, must be challenged for several reasons. First, our naïve understanding of space as geographically bounded and historically static containers of cultural difference can mask the mechanics of power (colonial projects being an obvious example). It can hide exactly how these ideas, which we take to be "natural," lead to the actual production of unequal power relations and difference, designating those who "deserve" to be treated well, and those who "deserve" to be treated as less-than-human. And when translated into sound and transmitted through national anthems or Hollywood film scores, the unequal power relations and problematic mobilizations of cultural difference we've explored here are powerfully (and often uncritically) inserted into our everyday lives.

Second, the notion of "absolute space" provides power-invested policymakers with rhetorical tools for attempts at civilizational self-justification and with a means of legitimizing imperialism and colonialism—space is either "advanced" and should be protected, or is "backwards" and available for colonization. Third, ideas about absolute space ignore the fluidity, complexity, historical dynamism, and tension *within* a so-called culture. And lastly, they do not account for the dynamic phenomena of migrations, which lead to constant cross-fertilization of supposedly unchanging cultures, musical and otherwise. When we take migration and the circulation of people and music into consideration, what kind of space might we hear?

2. Stirring up Absolute Space

Migration and Diaspora

While Hollywood's musical representations of "Africa" illustrate how sounds can reinforce the idea of absolute space, *Excursions* also offers plenty of musical case studies that challenge the idea of space as a static and uniform container of essentialized identity.

Space as a fixed and bounded concept is quickly destabilized when we consider migrations, cultural exchanges, and musical circulations across the world. Consider tango in Argentina, for example (see *Excursions*, Chapter 10). Tango is now a musical synonym for Argentina, the embodiment of national identity. But if we listen more closely, we hear that tango is inflected by the rural-to-urban labor migration of the mid-nineteenth century; the musical influences of Cuban *habanera* and African-derived *candombe*; and the international circulation of tango in the 1910s. Long decried by the country's elites and officials for its association with lower-class lifestyles, tango was not embraced as an embodiment of national essence until it gained popularity abroad. Heard this way, the nationalized space audible in tango is not a straightforward container for a coherent national identity, but rather a product of these dynamic, circuitous, and contested routes and movements of people, sound, and discourse.

These questions of space, music, and migration become even more compelling when we turn our ears to the Caribbean, a region of diasporic formations, where cultures reflect "the forced movement of ethnic groups from their homelands" (see *Excursions*, Chapter 11). Not only do Caribbean residents have their original roots in other places such as West Africa, Europe, South Asia, East Asia, and the Levant, but travel continues between the Caribbean, homelands, international metropoles like New York and London, and other diasporic clusters around the world. When there is such an active movement of people between the "home" country and diasporic locations, what kind of space is "home"? Does this term refer to your ancestral origin or to your present location? If your family has spread across diasporic locations, then where is, and what kind of space is, your "home"? And what kind of space is diaspora?

One musical answer, as we hear in the Bahamian song "Island Boy," is to consider the Caribbean a remembered and imagined "home," regardless of one's physical location in the diaspora. This creates a sense of space grounded in a discursive and experiential center, the nostalgic sense of a "good old home" in the Caribbean (the Bahamas, in this case) evoked through music. The space expressed in this example may resemble some of the parameters of absolute space—confinement of a stable identity within a national border (the Bahamas). But here, the singer's identity is not static and pre-existing, but explicitly constructed by the song, and the locale tied to this identity is not, in reality, bounded in the islands. Rather, it is a "Bahamas" created out of a layering of both imagined and physical space, that captures his longing for a sense of nostalgic "home"; the actual locales of the islands and metropoles; and the back-and-forth between those locations. It is a composite, multifaceted space that can only come into being because of the singer's movement across geographical boundaries.

Salsa further complicates the question of musical formations in and through diaspora. A richly multifaceted confluence of hybrid and flexible styles from Cuba and Puerto Rico that emerged in New York, salsa is an inherently diasporic music that has now achieved a global reach across Spanish-speaking Latin America and beyond. It has geographically grounded roots, but is also inherently transnational, without boundaries, physical confines, or a singular essentialized identity. Salsa's sounds initially highlight the movements, sentiments, and interactions among Caribbean and Latino musicians in New York, then traverse back to Latin America where they continue to produce this deeply diasporic space through further hybridized formations across national borders. The space produced through salsa, then, contests the very notion of "absolute space," in part because it is ever-shifting, dynamic, pluralistic, and always produced through movement and circulation.

For further exploration into the questions surrounding diaspora and music, I urge you to consult the "Music and Diaspora" chapter in this Reader. But diaspora is an important and compelling concept to think about when wrestling with music and space. However much musical sounds may be intended to represent a particular identity for a nation-state, musical practices like tango and salsa highlight how sound can encode cultural difference not as reified or monolithic, but rather as a product of ongoing, dynamic, and ceaselessly turbulent historical entanglements. I encourage you to keep asking: what kind of spatial understanding emerges from listening to the musical sounds that became possible because of the distinct histories of diasporic formations present in the Caribbean? Do you hear salsa as a music that moves across absolute space? Or does salsa, very much a music-in-constant-motion, create a different kind of space? What kind of space is diaspora? We will return to this question toward the end of this chapter.

3. Phenomenological Space and Soundscape

Embodiment, Class, and the Everyday

Thus far, I have used "space" even when describing examples of what you might usually call "places." Now, it is time to tease out some specific parameters for these two terms so that we can deploy them more critically in our thinking. One school of thought, which I will call "phenomenological space," differentiates the two this way: *space* is general and abstract, and becomes concrete and attains identity as a *place* through embodiment, experience, and groundedness. Put another way, place is space made meaningful through sensory experiences. Because music is a deeply embodied and sensorial practice, it plays a key role in turning mere "spaces" into "places" meaningful to humans.

Culturally specific practices of listening to sounds that are not conventionally considered "music" can also help us understand how people are socialized to understand and engage with the world sonically—to make space into place. Just as listening to crickets and cicadas is a cultivated aural sensibility to orient oneself temporally (to seasonal changes, for example) in Japan (see *Excursions*, Chapter 6), listening to sounds can be a way of attuning ourselves to the particular locale we are in.

45

Canadian composer R. Murray Schafer coined the term "soundscape" to conceptualize this approach to spatial orientation through sound (Schafer 1977 (1980)). Schafer suggested that, by privileging the acoustic dimension of our environment, we can gain a deeper appreciation for and understanding of a locality. Schafer himself had an ideological investment in upholding the "pure" sounds of nature untouched by human civilization, but many scholars of music and space have since critiqued the Western, Romantic ideal that presumes a binary separation between "human" and "nature." Schafer's "soundscape" concept also conflates sound and hearing. We must ask: does sound have an intrinsic meaning? Or do we find meanings through our hearing? For Schafer, certain ("natural") sounds are pure and worthy of protection, and certain ("polluting") sounds are best eliminated—assuming that sound has inherent values, to be perceived by careful listeners like himself—but do we all hear the same way? While Schafer called attention to the importance of listening as a way of engaging with the world, his idea of soundscape does not allow for the fact that we are all culturally conditioned to develop different ways of perceiving sound, and therefore, different interpretations and evaluations of sound.

With these caveats in mind, however, Schafer's call for attuning ourselves to the environment through listening has generated numerous new ways of producing knowledge about sound-space. Listening to sounds can help us get to know, and eventually navigate, a particular environment, especially if we are careful and aware of what assumptions we might be making as we pick up (or don't) on certain sounds. Next time you go out—whether around your own neighborhood or to a travel destination—you might want to try taking what Schafer called a "soundwalk," an excursion with the goal of listening to the environment.

Ouyang's sonic tour of everyday life in Taiwan is one good example of such a "soundwalk" (see *Excursions*, Chapter 4). Ouyang takes us on her stroll to a Taipei night market, on a subway ride, and on a jog in a park. We hear a few of what Schafer calls "soundmarks"—the acoustic equivalent of a landmark, a unique sound that identifies a particular place. For example, the sounds, smells, and humidity of Taipei's night markets all index the ways people socialize in the evening to escape from the heat, after long hours of work and school. Another example is one of the most well-known street sounds of Taipei: melodies played by garbage trucks. As Ouyang explains, well-organized and efficient waste management became a critical ecological and social mandate as Taiwan went through rapid industrialization. Listening to this iconic sound—or soundmark—gives us insight into the ecological, historical, and social forces at play in the everyday lives of Taipei's residents, helping us to understand this urban space as a "place."

The concept of soundscape, on the one hand, is fundamentally grounded in the notion of absolute space, as it assumes a geographically delineated understanding of static space with an intrinsic identity. On the other hand, however, soundscape highlights the productive potential of sound to help us experientially understand a particular locale, an environment, a territory—which in turn reveals social dynamics and histories that may not be immediately accessible to residents, let alone to casual visitors. However, it is important to ask: if phenomenological space becomes concrete through human perception, experience, and embodiment, does that assume the universality of such place-making experiences by all humans? And if so, does that mean all places are equally meaningful and powerful? Who has access to certain places, and to music? Who can hear this music? Do we all hear the same way? Who has the mobility and resources to move through places to experience their soundscapes?

One way to think about these questions is to ask who gets to control public soundscapes. We might consider how noise complaints rise dramatically in "gentrifying" areas of U.S. cities, as wealthier (often white) new residents encounter and are bothered by their (often black and Latinx) neighbors' amplified music that, whether played in apartments, on the stoop, or on the sidewalk, passes beyond private boundaries to create the neighborhood's soundscape. In 2019, such complaints temporarily shut down the go-go music that had projected for two decades from an electronics store in Shaw, an historically African-American neighborhood in Washington, DC. This dispute over whether residents in the neighborhood's new luxury apartments would have to listen to the blasting go-go, a homegrown DC hybrid music drawing on funk, R&B, and hip-hop—a "soundmark" of local identity—symbolizes the tension that can arise over soundscapes in densely populated areas with varying and changing demographics. It also illuminates how uneven power between communities can shape what we hear, or don't hear, every day.

4. Beyond Boundaries: Relational Space

Indigeneity, Environment, and Circulation

So far we have thought about space as an "absolute," a pre-given geographical unit that delineates cultural difference, which can then be claimed, owned, or controlled by particular people or groups. We have also thought about it in the realm of representation or imagination, like the "Africa" of stereotype or the "home" of diasporic migrants. And we have invoked the distinction some make between an inchoate "space" and a "place" created by human activity. Now, I want to introduce you to one last approach to thinking about space. What if humans do play a role in producing space, but not the *only* role? What if space is something that emerges from how we interact with and relate to other humans, non-human beings, and even objects around us, and through the histories that come with them?

Across musical practices among many North American indigenous groups, we learn about the indigenous orientation "toward the social, natural, and spiritual world that ... prioritizes the subject's place in a web of relations, and that ... reminds the subject ever to place her/himself in terms of that web of relations" (see *Excursions*, Chapter 12). But the "subjects" here, crucially, are not only human. Land is not an inert surface upon which actions take place, but one of many agents that, through interconnected relations with humans, animals, spirits, and other beings, co-produces the world. Three-dimensional space, understood in this light, is not a mere container or background for activity, but the dynamic product of human, animal, plant, and spirit interactions.

Sound, music, and dance play an essential role in forging these relationships. For instance, performance of songs, dances, and ceremonies is an important obligation when a person or group receives a gift from the spirits. In the traditional Nuu-chan-nulth practice of the Pacific Northwest, songs and dances are also a way of forging and reinforcing kinship relations; each family inherits, and owns, specific songs that perform this work. Cree and Ojibwe communities, whose lifeway involved seasonal migration, perform their communal bonds through regular meetings involving collective performances of song and dance. Powwows are spatial-musical processes through which nomadic or distant groups intersect spatially and reinforce or newly establish intertribal relationships, while also recognizing tribal differences and honoring community-specific responses to marginalization and oppression.

These examples highlight how music and sound are often neither an "expression" of the supposed inherent identity of a territory (absolute space), nor a simple observation of sounds tied to an environment (soundscape). Rather, music is, in these examples, a way of making sense of, and simultaneously making, the world, through relationships among multiple actors. Anthropologist Steven Feld (Feld 1996) coined the term "acoustemology" to describe a similar idea: sound as a way of knowing and being emplaced in the world. Feld's work with the Bosavi people in Papua New Guinea found that singing, hearing, and sounding are intrinsically integral to their way of knowing, as they navigate and create their world via singing and listening, and in active relationship to bird songs, to the spirits of those who have passed, to waterways, and to rainforests.

Space that is defined in such dynamic and interactive terms can be called "relational space." Cultural geographer Doreen Massey helps us think about relational space as extroverted, outward-looking, made up of historical encounters, and inclusive of interrelations among humans and non-human actors as well as the environment. Put another way, these actors don't just interact *within* space (conceived as a mere background or geographically bounded unit); space *comes into being* through dynamic relationships. And if we reframe our imagination of space as a "meeting-up of histories" and as "social relations stretched out," then space is revealed as inherently fluid and plural, since it's made up of historical encounters and multiple actors (Massey 2005: 4; 1994: 2). As an acoustic and social phenomenon that embodies and evokes histories and memories, sound and music is a powerful way to reorient our ears to listen for the extroverted aspects of relational space.

Japanoise provides an opportunity to hear such "extroverted" and relational space (see *Excursions*, Chapter 6). A cultural phenomenon that grew out of the circulation of small-scale experimental sounds from Japan to North America, it is a sound that emerged precisely through interconnections and circulations, both in imagination and on the ground. Layers of misunderstanding, projection, and un/mistranslation created unintended consequences and meanings, and Japanoise emerged out of this "cultural feedback." In this sound phenomenon, we hear, then, a deeply relational space that defies the characteristics of absolute space. Japanoise does not embody or represent the country or identity of "Japan," or of a singular musician, or group of musicians. Instead, it emerges in the back-and-forth oscillations of recordings, ideas, and performers, with sounds freed of any notion of physically bounded territory, and therefore devoid of any essentialized, stable identity. At once imaginary (imagination, misinterpretations, untranslation among North American fans) and concrete (recordings in the mail, underground experimental musicians in small venues of Kyoto and Osaka), Japanoise sounds out a relational space in and through relationships of global circulation.

You will probably hear echoes of the earlier discussion of diasporic music here; the sounds of salsa and tango engendered a space through the migration of people, the circulation of music, and the accompanying imaginations of "home" and different senses of belonging that these various movements precipitated. But, having added to our thinking the notion of relational and extroverted space, we can now raise slightly different questions about diaspora that nuance our understandings of the relationship between music and sound. Do you hear salsa as music that is moving within, and across, absolute space? Or does salsa *produce* an extroverted and relational space, arising from relations and interactions among people and environment across geographically delineated locales?

Summary

Just as ideas about music and sound vary throughout the world, our own implicit assumptions about how we understand "space" can be called into question. This chapter, the Reader it is part of, and *Excursions* itself, all seek to make you aware of the typical Western conception of space as only one possible approach among many. Such awareness allows us to observe and analyze music and sound with careful attention to how the intersection of sound and space affords us windows onto the intersection of power, culture, and difference. These intersections might take the form of appropriation or domination (as we've seen in our discussion of absolute space). But they can also lead to reification, contestation, or the creative or unintended formation of alliances and cultural forms (as we explored in our discussion of phenomenological space, diasporic space, and relational space).

And it is important to remember that these various ways of conceptualizing space are not mutually exclusive, but rather can overlap, support, or interrupt each other. We can, for instance, hold in mind a kind of absolute space (say, the geographic space of Hong Kong and the uniform history and identity assumed of its territory by the official narrative) even as we consider the relational spaces and the senses of "place" that are revealed and created by the sounds and music of the protest movement for the democratic future of that "absolute space" (see *Excursions*, Chapter 4). With this insight, I hope that you are able to expand your understanding of how sound and music work in relation to space; to hear the historical and political implications of different approaches to spatial thinking; and to explore new possibilities for hearing/understanding space through music.

If you haven't thought much about space and sound until now, it may feel challenging to wrap your head around some of these concepts. But listening to music, attending to sound, and exploring dance with critical attention are all powerful and compelling ways to explore different ways of thinking about (and experiencing) space. As you saw in the examples above, music can contribute to producing a misconceived sense of space, depriving it of the lived realities of the actual inhabitants. Music can also be mobilized to symbolize a supposedly essentialized and unitary identity within a given territory. But even in such cases, sounds can also tell us a lot about the entangled histories of cultural exchanges and relationships that might contradict false narratives of cultural uniformity and historical stasis. Sound can also uncover deeper insights into what you might take for granted in your everyday environment. Or, instead of being something that happens in or through space, music can be an agent that produces an active, extroverted space through its interaction with the environment, humans, and other actors.

Music and sound play a profound role in providing a sense of who we are in the world, how we move through the world, and how we orient ourselves toward others and the environment. Music, sound, and dance help us hear the multiple qualities, types, properties, and attributes of space and attend to its relationality. On any musical excursion, either in your everyday life or to an unfamiliar place, you might try to listen and ask: what kinds of stories, memories, histories, relationships, and forces are audible in this space? Which ones might be suppressed, blocked, silenced, or excluded? What kind of space is being sounded out through them? What are the repercussions and consequences of different ways of understanding space? And how might music and sound offer a way not only to understand them, but to create new possibilities?

References

Feld, Steven. 1996. "Waterfalls of Song: An Acoustemology of Place Resounding in Bosavi, Papua New Guinea." In *Senses of Place*, edited by Steven Feld and Keith H. Basso, 91–136. Santa Fe, NM: School of American Research Advanced Seminar Series.

Massey, Doreen. 1994. *Space, Place and Gender*. Minneapolis, MN: University of Minnesota Press.

Massey, Doreen. 2005. *For Space*. London: Sage.

Said, Edward. 1978. "Imaginative Geography and Its Representations: Orientalizing the Oriental." In *Orientalism*, 49–72. New York: Vintage Books.

Schafer, R. Murray. 1977 (1980). *The Turning of the World: Toward a Theory of Soundscape Design*. Philadelphia, PA: University of Pennsylvania Press.

Smith, Neil, and Cindy Katz. 1993. "Grounding Metaphor: Towards a Spatialized Politics." In *Place and the Politics of Identity*, edited by M. Keith and S. Pile. London: Routledge.

6

MUSIC AND DIASPORA

Timothy Rommen

Have you ever really thought about the freedom of movement that many of us, especially those of us hailing from the North Atlantic, enjoy? Whether travelling internationally with family at the holidays; joining friends for a quick vacation in a popular tourist destination; or, perhaps, studying abroad for a semester—your citizenship status (especially if it is granted by the "right" nation-state) can come with profoundly enabling privileges related to mobility. I would venture to guess that at least some of you have had the luxury of not needing to think a great deal about how much access and protection your passport gives you, or about how relatively easy it is for you to obtain everything from student visas to entry on a tourist visa. We do, of course, need the requisite resources to travel, and so the mobility I'm referencing here is also a matter of class (and this is no small issue in a world where the wealth gap is so severe and resources distributed so very unevenly). But that is a subject for another essay. My point here is more about what it means to have, at the very least, the theoretical possibility for such mobility. For this possibility is not shared by everyone. National borders are permeable for some but hard as stone for others. Sometimes they work much better in one direction than the other. Immigration policies impinge upon and block many who are simply trying to move toward a vision of their future just as you and I are doing in our own ways.

The bottom line here is that many of us, myself included, have the luxury of traversing borders, mostly freely, and of pursuing our interests, careers, and education more or less how and where we choose. Throughout history, however, many people have moved around the world not freely but rather because they were compelled to do so, either by force (slavery, exile), or because of political, religious, social, or economic factors beyond their control (war, religious persecution, violence, famine). In this short essay, I'd like to explore how music travels with individuals and communities who find themselves far from "home" and working to rebuild life in new places. I'd like to do this by first introducing the concept of diaspora and then offering a few examples taken from *Excursions in World Music* to illustrate how powerful music can be in these circumstances. I'll also consider why thinking with diaspora affords us insights that we would likely not generate if we focus only on migration and mobility.

Diaspora

Diaspora, a Greek word meaning, roughly, "to scatter about," has historically been a useful way of referencing the mass movements of people out of their traditional homelands and into new territories, generally by force, and usually without the possibility of a return. The desire for a return, the pain and nostalgia that accompany such longing in the face of the existential reality of permanent exile from one's home, and the necessity and difficulty of building life anew in a new place, despite such conditions, are all foundational to the experience of diaspora. This term was initially deployed within the academy in order to describe the dispersal of Jews around the world. During the twentieth century, it also became a common framework within which to think about the Armenian diaspora (which I will not have space to discuss here) and the African diaspora (of which more below). Within the Jewish tradition, there is, perhaps, no more iconic illustration of the sense of dislocation and sorrow that accompanies diaspora than the well-known text of Psalm 137:

> By the rivers of Babylon—there we sat down and there we wept
> when we remembered Zion.
> On the willows there we hung up our harps.
> For there our captors asked us for songs,
> and our tormentors asked for mirth, saying,
> "Sing us one of the songs of Zion!"
> How could we sing the Lord's song in a foreign land?
>
> (NRSV Psalm 137: 1–4)

It is no accident that music is part of the calculus here. Do you have any songs in your life that index a place (or perhaps a memory) you hold dear? If you do, would it be appropriate to play those songs just anywhere, or do they hold a special place for you that should be taken into account when performing them? As Psalm 137 tells it, the Jewish community exiled in Babylon felt it incongruous, if not impossible, to sing the songs of Zion (or Jerusalem) in that place—"how could we sing the Lord's song in a foreign land?" As we will see, music plays a powerful role not only in remembering and celebrating "home," but also in the gradual, intergenerational reconfiguration of a diasporic space into a place where life can be celebrated again.

A good example of this process can be seen in the African diaspora. You may know that an adaptation of Psalm 137 was written by the Jamaican reggae band, The Melodians, in 1970 and included on the soundtrack for the film *The Harder They Come* in 1972. Called "Rivers of Babylon," the song offers a particularly powerful example of Rastafari religious worldviews, a multilayered historical commentary on slavery and colonialism, and a political message pointing out continued oppression even in newly postcolonial Jamaica (independent since 1962). Just a few points here: within Rastafari thought, the historical city of

Babylon is reconfigured to refer to the colonial system (Babylon system) but also to the diasporic spaces (like Jamaica) into which African slaves were transported. Zion here refers not to Jerusalem, but to Ethiopia, which, in Rastafari thought, is the promised land. The history of diaspora indexed in The Melodians' version of Psalm 137 includes experiences of the middle passage and slavery, the various means by which colonial law and policy maintained degrees of unfreedom and inequality even after emancipation, and the extent to which even postcolonial, independent Jamaica is subject to neocolonial influence. Here's how The Melodians rework Psalm 137:

> By the rivers of Babylon [Jamaica]—where he sat down,
> and there he wept when he remembered Zion [Ethiopia].
> 'Cause the wicked [slavers, colonial officials, plantation owners,
>   International Monetary Fund].
> carried us away captivity [slavery as well as post-slavery colonial/
>   neocolonial/postcolonial forms of unfreedom],
> Required from us a song.
> How can we sing King Alpha's [Rastafari reference to King Haile
>   Selassie] song in a strange land?

What becomes clear, as we compare this example to the text of Psalm 137, are the ways that The Melodians invest the lyrics not just with different meanings, but also with references to a much more sweeping historical trajectory and political landscape than does the original text. And I believe that we can see, in this example, a journey from diaspora to home. What I mean here is that, articulated from the perspective of an independent Jamaica in 1970, these lyrics provide a rich and multilayered lesson in diasporic life. We can interpret them as memorializing the experiences of slaves in a new place (the experiences of the band's distant ancestors). But these lyrics also index the plight of unequal subjects in a colonial, post-slavery Jamaica (including the plight of their parents). Finally, we can also hear in these words a contemporary protest over the inequalities that obtain in a neocolonial, independent Jamaica (their Jamaica) in which it is still appropriate to sing about Babylon, Zion, the wicked, and captivity. What has changed isn't the *fact* of diaspora, but rather the sense that Jamaica is now "home"—if an imperfect and complicated one—and more home than Zion (Ethiopia), which exists more as a metaphor/aspiration in Rastafari faith than as a concrete possibility. The weight of generation upon generation living in and making life work in Jamaica, and doing so without access to ancestral homelands, necessarily changes the way that diaspora is experienced over time.

And the Caribbean, in particular, is a collection of sites in which most everyone is from somewhere else—some by choice, many more by force (see *Excursions*, Chapter 11). It is also a space within which musicians, playwrights, dancers, religious leaders, and many others have identified ways to start "singing the Lord's [or King Alpha's] song in a [no longer] strange land." These songs have taken a variety of forms: some traditions have resisted colonial impositions, others have created hybrid or creolized practices; all have required coming to terms with diaspora.

Think for a minute about the difficult choices that many slaves would have had to make with regard to religious practice. Having been torn from their own communities, their religious traditions, and the contexts within which such worship and devotion became socially meaningful, slaves were introduced to Christianity by the very people who enslaved them(!). The irony of this absurd and deeply tragic situation notwithstanding, many slaves did accommodate themselves to one degree or another to the new religion. But this didn't preclude them from also holding on to what they could of their past religious practices, including the songs, the rituals, and the social organizations they enabled, thus giving rise to a great variety of sacred traditions that variously resist, combine with, or oppose Catholic and Protestant practices. The results are musically diverse and existentially and spiritually rich and include *vodoun* (Haiti), *santería* (Cuba), obeah (Bahamas), shango (Trinidad), and myal, convince, and Rastafarianism (Jamaica), to name just a few. These practices tend to hold in view both African antecedents and Caribbean realities, marking them as creole—which, in this context, means that they combine ideas from multiple sources into a new practice indebted to, but distinct from, the original practices.

This sense of being both African and Jamaican, or African and Trinidadian (of having multiple, competing sources for one's identity), has been identified by W.E.B. Du Bois, in the context of the United States, as a hallmark of diasporic existence. Du Bois called this recognition of multiplicity "double consciousness." Paul Gilroy, writing about this idea, puts it this way:

> Double consciousness was initially used to convey the special difficulties arising from black internalisation of an American identity: "One ever feels his twoness, an American, a Negro; two souls, two thoughts, two unreconciled strivings; two warring ideals in one dark body whose dogged strength alone keeps it from being torn asunder." However, I want to suggest that Du Bois produced this concept ... not just to express the distinctive standpoint of black Americans but also to illuminate the experience of post-slave populations in general.
>
> (1993: 126)

The idea of creolization is one way in which such multiplicities were confronted, absorbed, and reframed to create cultural productions (music, dance, theater, carnival, etc.) that reflected the new realities that each successive generation confronted in these places that gradually became "homes." In their very formation, however, these cultural productions bear the traces of diasporic experience. The combination of African, European, and, in some cases, Amerindian elements (instruments, aesthetics, etc.) in the creation of such creole musics betrays the long history, stretching over five centuries, of interaction, exchange, and coexistence (if unequal and complicated by what The Melodians call the "wicked") in the Caribbean.

As just one example among many, I point you to rake 'n' scrape in the Bahamas (see *Excursions*, Chapter 11). This music, originally developed to accompany social dancing, rose to prominence in the Bahamas during the late nineteenth and early twentieth centuries. A creole or creolized musical style, rake 'n' scrape is based on a combination of European and African instruments (accordion and goatskin drum) and on a successful combination of European and African conceptions of embodied rhythm (several European dances, along with African dances, all accompanied by the predominantly African-derived rhythms played on the drum). Today, the traditional form is primarily considered a heritage music, but its rhythms inform a popular music of the same name that continues to attract new artists and audiences. In the end, rake 'n' scrape is a creole musical tradition, neither African nor European, but rather Caribbean—specifically, Bahamian. It is also a musical tradition that could only have emerged in and through the experiences, dislocations, and re-groundings of diasporic life.

Diaspora: Other Possibilities

During the late twentieth century, scholars began to expand the use of diaspora to include many other possibilities. Kevin Kenney, a diaspora studies scholar and historian, has this to say about this shift:

> The dismantling of European empires inspired new forms of transnational solidarity, especially among people of African descent. Decolonization also led to the displacement of certain migrant populations in various parts of Asia and Africa. Involuntary migrants classified as refugees received international recognition and protection, bringing global attention to the idea of diaspora. The number of international migrants increased dramatically in recent decades. New forms of technology facilitated faster international travel and communication. And national governments began to reach out in new ways to their overseas populations in search of economic and political support. These developments help explain not only why the term diaspora has become so popular but also why it is used in such a wide variety of ways.

(2013: 9)

Thinking with Kenney, it becomes possible to see why the South Asian diaspora in the United Kingdom and the United States, for instance, or any similar community living outside of their historical homeland, is now likely to be described as diasporic. One of the fundamental differences between such uses of the concept and the more iconic examples I discussed in the previous section, however, is that there usually exists for individuals in these communities a possibility of return to their homeland. In fact, frequent travel back and forth is common. It is also the case that many of these communities (though not all—refugees, for instance) have moved by choice, perhaps in search of educational or professional opportunities, and then stayed "abroad" in their new hostland. This is not to negate the deep feelings of longing for "home" or the sense of dislocation and isolation that can and do accompany such migrations, but we should acknowledge that such a use of diaspora is qualitatively different from how it has been experienced and what it has meant for the Jewish or African diasporas. That said, there is much we can learn by expanding the scope of diaspora to include such communities, and it shouldn't come as a surprise that music plays an important role in these cases as well.

For instance, there are, in Maritime Southeast Asia, several such diasporic communities (see *Excursions*, Chapter 7). I'd like to highlight just one of them here. In his discussion of the Malay world, Jim Sykes introduces a non-Malay population called the Straits Chinese (also known as the Baba-Nonya). This population, numbering about eight million and spread all across Indonesia, Malaysia, Singapore, and Thailand, is descended from early Chinese migrants and has adopted Malay customs and several Malay creole languages (called Baba Malay). In adapting to life in new places around Maritime Southeast Asia, many of these Straits Chinese chose to adopt as their own a Malay musical practice called *pantun*, a kind of improvised sung poetry that, as Sykes explains, can be sung on its own or *within* certain musical genres. The Straits Chinese favored singing pantuns within a genre called *dondang sayang* ("Love Song"), which involves men and women improvising witty and flirtatious pantuns to one another. As Sykes notes,

> at least until the 1960s, Straits Chinese families were known to hold dondang sayang sessions in their private homes for families and friends; and pantuns by that point were sung not only in the Baba Malay creole but also sometimes in Hokkien, the language from southern China.

Here then, we see a local Malay genre adapted to the needs of a non-Malay population, sung in different contexts, and even in a different language, as a community came to terms with the contours of its diasporic life.

But it is also important to consider how, as a community deals with the exigencies of diaspora, it can also connect with other, similar communities in a new place, using the musical ideas it has brought with it as a foundation from which to develop new, diasporic practices. I'd like to show you how we can both "see" and "hear" such diasporic connections. Good examples of this can be found in new York City's Labor Day Parade (see *Excursions*, Chapter 11), and in the development of salsa music, also in New York City (see *Excursions*, Chapter 10). From at least the turn of the twentieth century, New York City was an attractive destination for both West Indian (think here of people hailing from the English-speaking Caribbean—from places such as Trinidad, Jamaica, and Guyana) and Latinx migrants. People moved to pursue educational opportunities, for work, or to join family already living in New York City. And, even though long-standing national and regional rivalries existed between the various West Indian communities, in the context of New York City, West Indians had much more in common with other West Indians than with the white, U.S. American population. The same was true of the various Latinx communities arriving in New York City: whether hailing from Puerto Rico, the Dominican Republic, Cuba, or nations in Central and South America, these communities, too, had more in common with each other in the context of New York City than they might have acknowledged at "home." And this realization makes new diasporic solidarities and affinities possible. But how do these new solidarities look and sound?

Perhaps the most visible example I can point to is the annual Labor Day Parade, which is a West Indian-inspired carnival. At "home" in the Caribbean, fierce rivalries exist (have you ever seen a soccer match between Trinidad and Jamaica?), but in New York City, West Indians recognize the utility, visibility, and strength that numbers can provide. As such, those regional rivalries (we are Trinidadian, or Jamaican) remain important but are nested within the larger diasporic identity (we are West Indians) necessitated by living in New York City. So, the West Indian community comes out and participates in the Labor Day Parade en masse, but you will still see Jamaican, Trinidadian, and Guyanese flags flying proudly even as revelers assert their solidarity as West Indians.

But we can also "hear" the growth of such diasporic affinities and solidarities by attending to musical exchanges. So, let's think, briefly, about what listening to salsa can help us understand about the Latinx community. Since at least the 1930s, a series of musical interactions between Cuban master drummers, Puerto Rican musicians, Dominican players, and jazz artists, produced a series of musical constellations, including the Cu-bop of the 1940s, the Latin Big Band scene of the 1950s (think cha-cha-chá and mambo), and the Boogaloo craze of the 1960s (which was, in its own way, also a profound interaction with African-American musical styles which I don't have space to address here). Salsa emerged out of this constantly hybridizing context in the 1970s, absorbing a bit of all that had preceded it into its own sound and aesthetic approach. It is, as such, a sound with multiple sources—it is no longer possible to hear salsa as Cuban or Puerto Rican. Instead, it is a musical style that emerged in and through the processes of diaspora.

In fact, one important way to "hear" salsa is as a cultural production that is only possible because it has developed in multiple diasporic contexts. The roots of salsa completed the middle passage in the hearts and minds of unfree African musicians and dancers and then grew into important diasporic musical traditions like bomba, plena (Puerto Rico), rumba, and son (Cuba), to name but a few. These musical traditions, carried in the hearts and minds of now free but still diasporic Afro-Caribbean musicians and dancers, travelled throughout the twentieth century to a new diasporic destination—to New York City, that is. In a profound way, then, what we hear when we listen to salsa is music that bears, in its core aesthetic principles, the memory and consequences of two very different kinds of diasporic experience.

58

Migration or Diaspora? Sounds and People on the Move

But couldn't the examples in the previous section (Straits Chinese, Labor Day Parade, salsa) be productively described and analyzed through the lens of migration and mobility instead of through diaspora? I think that the answer here is an equivocal "yes and no." In one sense, diaspora merely helps us think about specific instances of migration. It helps us think about communities moving across the globe, forming new connections and facing new challenges and opportunities in new places. This entire essay is, at this level, certainly about migration and a range of involuntary and voluntary mobilities. And yet, I think diaspora remains especially useful for focusing attention on the networks that extend beyond the binary of home and abroad, or homeland and hostland. Let's look again at the three case studies I briefly introduced above.

In the case of the Straits Chinese, this population of some 8 million people is dispersed across the Malay world—a geography that, today, is divided between several nation-states, including Indonesia, Malaysia, Singapore, and Thailand. What thinking with diaspora can offer here that migration is less able to highlight are the networks of belonging and shared identity that extend across these various "national" boundaries, connecting the Straits Chinese in their various hostlands to each other as well as maintaining links (though not necessarily loyalty) to their ancestral homeland of China.

The Labor Day Parade in New York City can be read, from the perspective of migration, as a continuation of culturally relevant practices developed in West Indian homeland(s) in a new hostland. What diaspora adds here is a fine-grained analysis of the ways that the idea of West Indian is mobilized and a recognition of the discrete identities that it folds into its collective in the process. But, if we think beyond the specifics of the New York City scene, diaspora also offers ways of thinking about how the Labor Day Parade is connected to and in dialogue with similar celebrations such as the Notting Hill Carnival and Caribana, held annually in London and Toronto, respectively. What diaspora adds to the discourse of migration, then, is the ability to think carefully about how these nodes in far-flung networks of diasporic communities interact, support each other, become rivals to each other, and reflect ever-changing relationships to homelands in the Caribbean.

Finally, salsa, too, is better thought in terms of diaspora. Let me continue the story of salsa from where I had left off earlier. Although the 1970s saw the birth of salsa as we understand it today, it didn't stay confined to audiences in New York City. In fact, in large part because of the profoundly diasporic roots of the genre, salsa was rapidly exported to other locations, including to Colombia, Venezuela, and many other locations throughout Central and South America, where communities were readily able to identify with the music and dance. Thus, while migration and mobility certainly help us explore some of salsa's journeys, diaspora enables us to think about the deep connections and historical solidarities that can be shared, in this case, through a musical genre. Put differently, the very fact that salsa is a diasporic musical formation is, in fact, one of the reasons for its migrations across the Americas—one of the reasons that people from Cali to Caracas recognized themselves in its sounds and movements. And in so doing, new diasporic nodes became a part of a larger network that is better captured by the concept of diaspora than by migration.

I should point out here that the three examples I have chosen to highlight in this essay represent only a fraction of the diasporic communities and musics discussed in *Excursions in World Music*. You will encounter many rich examples as you read your textbook and I hope that this short essay has given you some tools for reading about and exploring these histories of migration, mobility, and diasporic life. I'll leave you with a few questions to consider as you continue thinking about diaspora.

How should we think about refugee communities who live in hostlands far removed from their homelands and without the ability to return? Think here of Syrian refugees hoping for the chance to escape war and make life anew/again in Europe. They are migrants, yes, but their experiences and musical practices might be better thought through the lens of diaspora. Or, how do we address the increasingly restrictive immigration policies sweeping into vogue around Europe and in the United States? Where does this leave migrants who are hoping to make a new life in a new place? And how do we reconcile all of this with the fact that the migrants (and refugees) most disproportionally affected in all of this tend not to be white and often hail from the Global South? These migrants (and refugees, too) are literally caught between hostland and homeland, unable to live in either. The inequities begin to pile up. Or, how do we understand communities, like the West Indian or Latinx community in New York City, who at one and the same time appreciate their place in a new hostland but also remain connected to and invested in relationships that extend far beyond the nation-state in which they currently live? All of these questions reflect the complexities of diasporic experience. And all of these complexities are rehearsed and explored through music, dance, art, and poetry—that is, in the cultural productions that enliven and sustain these communities. And this is perhaps the primary reason why ethnomusicologists continue to engage urgently with questions of diaspora as they spend time thinking with communities about what it means to "sing the Lord's song in a foreign land."

References

Gilroy, Paul. 1993. *The Black Atlantic: Modernity and Double Consciousness*. Cambridge, MA: Harvard University Press.

Kenney, Kevin. 2013. *Diaspora: A Very Short Introduction*. New York: Oxford University Press.

7

COMMUNICATION, TECHNOLOGY, MEDIA

Andrea F. Bohlman

Questioning Listening

I'll begin by posing a simple, but hard, thought question. Think about your life over the last twenty-four hours. When did you hear music? Perhaps you were intentional in the first moments that spring to mind. Maybe you connected some headphones to a mobile device and chose some music to listen to while you exercised, commuted, or worked. Or you participated in a live rehearsal with an ensemble, turned on the radio while cooking, sat down to do an assignment for the class for which you purchased this Reader. Or maybe you huddled over a cell phone to watch a streaming music video suggested by a family member or friend, whether through social media or in person. You might have attended a concert or watched a video of a performance on television.

These are all modes of purposefully accessing music and directing your ears and body to it as an object that is, more or less, at the center of your experience of the world. The tasks that clear time to focus upon the sound of music unfolding—things like cooking, driving to work, the repetition that goes into practicing for a performance—help to frame the thing you are listening to as music, too. You configure yourself for desired acoustics by cutting off other sounds with headphones, enclosing yourself in a car, shutting the door to a room, hovering over a piano, and picking a track that will choreograph your running or dancing legs. Often, when we notice music in our lives, it's not only because we are listening, but because we have to work to foster a relationship to it. We set aside time for it and, sometimes unconsciously, orchestrate how it resonates: what technologies and materials bring it to life.

I might have asked a different, but also hard, leading question to invite you into the issues raised by this chapter: what are some remarkable sounds you heard over the last twenty-four hours? Some of these might be easily categorized as music: the sound track to a video game that sticks in your ear, the song you've set to play as your morning wake-up alarm, the DJ mixing tracks in the apartment above or below you, or the street musician you walked by as you got off a bus to do some errands. These listening experiences might have stimulated in you some of the same emotional and physical responses as those intentional musical encounters you recalled in response to my first question: feelings like calm, focus, frustration, and excitement. Maybe you sang or danced along. Your floor vibrated; your pulse quickened. Maybe you think of these interruptions as music, but they communicate differently than the music you "made space for"—the music over which you had power—in the first exercise. You did not set the terms of engagement for your encounter with these sounds: they accompany, interrupt, intrude, and distract you. Some of this music is called noise—or its makers are called noisy. Noise is a term which emphasizes that in these contexts, this sound is less valued and even unwanted.

Why and how we encounter sound—its context—influences what we call it, how we listen to it, and what it communicates to us. When we call something we hear a sound, it does not carry the same set of cultural meanings that the very same thing can have when we call it music. Interpreting something we hear (or make) as music is a means of distinction, a way of separating something apart and often above the wider, presumably more neutral, concept of sound. The collection of musical noises I conjured here in response to the second listening question serves as a reminder that music is often present in our lives even when we do not prioritize it, or are not necessarily aware of it consciously. In fact, it is very likely that most of the music you hear is not the product of you pushing a button, turning up the volume, plugging in headphones, turning on your amp, or tuning up your instrument. But you probably still cherish some of these sounds, whether because they are familiar, comforting, intriguing, or delightfully surprising. They shape your home, your hobbies, your everyday life. Music is not only there when we explicitly tune in: it is embedded in the spaces through which we move. We bring it into the world; the world mediates it to us. The "how" of this mediation is what the study of communication, technology, and media dwells upon, from the myriad of means of sound production to the feelings produced in individuals and across communities when they hear that sound.

Note that my second leading question wasn't about music, it was about remarkable sounds. So maybe you would answer that question along completely different lines than those that guided my suggestions. The bark of your pet dog when you were out walking at night made you notice a neighbor across the street on a very similar routine stroll. A clanking radiator in your apartment building roused you out of a deep slumber and made you grumpy. You made a telephone call just to hear a comforting voice. You are learning a new language, and you spend time in the morning making faces in the mirror to get the "l" sound just right. At the end of the day, you opened a cold beverage and sat outside, listening to the buzzing sound of summer insects and a game of pick-up basketball nearby. You rode a subway or bus that was so noisy, you put on headphones—and closed your eyes—just to shut out the sound.

All of us could make our own versions of this list, paying attention (as I have) to our bodies and psychological responses as much as to the vibrating matter or digital technology out of which the sound originates. Crucially, who we are and what our life has been like impacts not just *what* is on the list, but *how* we describe and relate to these sounds. As I shared my hypothetical list, I foregrounded the meanings deduced from each sound: what it communicated to me. There is a science to sound: we can measure pitch, volume, and duration, for example. Much of the technology that enables us to reproduce music was developed in the late nineteenth century to study sound along these parameters. But, as you can see across all of the examples I have evoked thus far, much of what sound and music communicate to us is a product of our cultural experiences and cannot be easily measured by others or by devices. When we study music as communication, music technologies, and musical media, we are questioning how we ourselves—but also how other people—listen so that we might better understand the always shifting interface between our individual lives and the broader value systems and infrastructures that are products of culture *through sound*.

Keep a sound diary for just one day, incessantly asking yourself what you hear. You will be overwhelmed by the quantity of information and meaning that sound conveys to you. (Indeed, this is one way in which the infrastructures and social structures of twenty-first century life privilege hearing individuals.) Music and sound are constantly there in the world around us, and we are constantly making decisions to pay attention or turn away. As we feel, we think about how what we hear relates to what we see, taste, touch, and smell, building our sensorium. Sound is *mediated* when it travels as vibrations through materials. Membranes on drums and in our ears—both *technologies*—vibrate, as do molecules of air in between. The sounds and music we hear always *communicate* across a gap between ourselves (as listeners—even when we are also performers) and the cultural contexts to which we are relating.

Thinking about music along the themes of technology, communication, and media emphasizes what scholars call the relationality of music: its profound capacity to shape connections. Music and sound are the result of actions and they prompt action: at a protest someone might shout "No justice, no peace!" and the rest of the crowd joins in chorus. On the dance floor, someone might mouth "come join me," while making eye-contact with their partner as they strut over—to the beat—to move their bodies in tandem. These kinds of relationships formed through sound are not just the domain of human interaction. Sound connects non-humans and humans: dogs hear dogs bark, too. It shapes our social relationships to things: we ask our cell phones questions by speaking to them. By ourselves, we tease music out of the strings of a guitar with our hands—sometimes in that moment, we feel least alone. The feelings we have as a result of music and sound are the result of their communicative power. Technology, communication, and media are closely linked concepts of central importance for making and studying music. When we focus on them, we learn about how music moves among people, how it is shared, and how knowledge about music is transmitted. The rest of this chapter grounds these terms in their specific meanings, providing examples of what kinds of questions they raise about what music is and how we listen.

Communication

Music and sound communicate because they convey information and organize social contact. The word communication is used to describe the action of making something common or shared: I communicate to you. In contemporary usage, it also refers to the object, in this case, the sound, that is shared: this is my communication. The information that sound and music convey depends on many factors: how is the sound made? What does it sound like (which is, of course, a matter of opinion)? And, crucially, who is listening? The latter question unleashes a whole new set of questions: what does the listener know? Why, when, and how are they listening? When studying music, we have tended to ask these questions about human listeners, thinking about how music and sound create shared knowledge among people through their capacity to communicate. But people also make music for divine audiences and as divine offerings. Non-human animals—such as frogs, whales, and cicadas—respond to the vibrations of sound, too, as they communicate among each other, or respond to changes in their environment like rain and fire.

Asking questions about the listener, however, does draw attention to *human* difference, while also showing how musical communication is often a common, or mutual, process: a two-way street. Perhaps you, as you read the opening section of this Reader chapter, dwelled on how the examples I offered diverged from your own responses. There are biological differences that are a factor of age—generally our ears hear a smaller range of pitches and struggle to attend to quieter sounds as we grow older—and human variance. Differences abound as a result of where we are born, what languages (and how many) we speak, and what and how much musical training we have undertaken, just as examples. The communities to which we have belonged—their musics, cultural values, and ritual traditions—configure our own sets of norms and expectations for listening. For example, in many black Pentecostal worship contexts in the United States, a preacher's sermon is considered powerful if the speaker's voice is resonant, loud, and dramatic. However, within mass in the Latin American Roman Catholic Church, the priest is expected to keep his voice unremarkable so as not to distract from the text of his homily. In his chapter on "Music of the Middle East and North Africa," Richard Jankowsky discusses how the ethical implications of listening, as an "active endeavor," have been central to many Islamic traditions because of the central importance of the recitation of the Qur'an (see *Excursions*, Chapter 3).

Thinking of music and sound together is critical for thinking about music as communication. To call something music is not just to elevate it, it is to impute a cultural assumption upon it and, in the process, begin to define what the nature of this sound's communication is. Our ears, no matter how capable they are of hearing, do not instinctively distinguish music from sound. It is our brains, upon perceiving sound, that process the signals according to the cultural knowledge that we have acquired. That knowledge orders and organizes the loud and quiet, dangerous and soothing, resonant and dry, repetitive and intermittent sounds around us. A key takeaway from the textbook that this Reader accompanies is *how* music and sound are understood and valued differently around the world. On the way, as you read about difference and across difference, I encourage you to articulate the ideas about hearing and understanding sound you hold implicitly.

Technology

In the twenty-first century, the idea of technology conjures up innovation and certain kinds of objects. Music technologies like noise-cancelling headphones, a surround-sound home entertainment center, and sonically immersive virtual reality gaming environments come to mind. These are all digital audio interfaces (often with moving images) made possible through relatively recent engineering breakthroughs, cherished because of their possibility. That is to say that in everyday use, there is a common equivalence of technology and technological progress that emphasizes the power of technology—maybe even over us. Technology, here, is misconstrued as a thing outside of culture that has effects upon people and the environments in which we live, but has a life of its own.

Skeptics of technology, more often than not, also operate on the terms and conditions of this reifying definition, as they express their worries about what effects new technologies will have on social life—and musical culture. When, in 1877, Thomas Edison developed an instrument to record sound onto wax cylinders for playback (an invention that is often counted as the "beginning" of sound recording), critics were anxious that sound recording would ultimately supplant live musical performance, threatening elite concert series and amateur music making alike. This concern that recorded sound is not as good, full, or authentic as "live" performance has been repeated and varied over the last century and a half, often to make claims that a certain kind of music is lesser or that a particular performer is less musical. The tradition of karaoke that Joshua Pilzer discusses in his chapter on Korea has many Western critics who frame the creatively vibrant and socially intimate practice of singing oneself into the sounds of cherished popular music as a problem (see *Excursions*, Chapter 5). These detractors scoff that karaoke musicians are dependent on technology— karaoke machines—to make bad copies of other people's music rather than forming their own bands and writing their own songs. This critique categorically dismisses technological reproduction as artificial, with the larger repercussion of reinforcing a Western hegemony that privileges authors (over performers) as the most creative artists. Other examples of the prestige and uniqueness accorded live music, under the presumption it is less mediated and therefore more authentic, abound. When a mainstream pop star is "caught" lip synching at a stadium concert, they are frequently scorned for depending on technology to complete their act. When the Metropolitan Opera of New York started simulcasting its Saturday afternoon matinees to movie theaters around the world—certainly a gesture that increased access to that elite art form—the video productions were scrutinized for ways they diverged from stage productions that, for example, depend on the acoustics of the hall for amplification instead of the live mixing efforts of sound recordists.

There is no denying that technology influences our lives. As a part of culture, it is *implicated* in power relations. Many global music traditions use notation to represent sounds visually. Lead sheets give jazz musicians access to chord progressions for songs they are performing, so they don't have to memorize a whole set and so they can teach and share their compositions. At the same time, notation can be a gatekeeper that prevents access—in this case for musicians without jazz literacy—to repertories. Digital devices, like hearing aids, and technological possibilities, like closed captioning, provide deaf communities access to music and sound. They require constant maintenance, some of which can only be done by technicians. The undersea cables that wire information—like phone calls and digital video—across oceans help music circulate globally, collapsing distances with their high-speed connectivity. As listeners, we think we can hear music from anywhere because we have an internet connection. (Plenty of music is not online.) Of course, one must have an internet connection in order to stream or download: the access that technology provides almost always also highlights economic inequalities that follow the geography of colonialism and are exacerbated by the power of corporations. When we study music technology, we must also analyze commerce: how money shapes which artists get promoted on mass media such as radio, television, and streaming services, for instance.

Another way of defining technology, drawn from its etymology, directs our attention to the materials out of which music is made (including the human larynx, itself a technology). The word is derived from the Greek, *techné*, which referred to an art or craft—something that gets your hands dirty instead of the abstracted thinking of philosophy or politics. Since the nineteenth century, technology has referred to the practical application of science—fields such as chemistry, acoustics, electrical engineering, and computing have had strong influences on music's technologies. One important contribution of this way of thinking about technology is that it emphasizes the fact that musical instruments are some of the most ubiquitous—certainly over the course of global history—musical technologies. As you engage with *Excursions*, notice how frequently studying a musical tradition begins with understanding how musical instruments are played, how they sound, and how they constitute social groups. Some instruments are more complicated than others, some have changed over time—as they migrated to new climates or to differently constituted musical ensembles; as different raw materials were extracted and processed into rubber, plastic, and more; or as advances in engineering opened up new creative potentials.

This is not to say that technological possibility determines what music is made, or that a more complex technology produces better music. Think about the difference between an electric guitar, a ukulele, an acoustic guitar, and a banjo. They have sound worlds so divergent, to say one is better than another seems absurd. This despite the similarities in the skill sets performers bring to performances on all four (strumming, picking out melodies, and providing an accompanying texture). One, the banjo, has its origins in the Atlantic slave trade. One, the electric guitar, is a towering representation of rock'n'roll's masculine power. One, the ukulele, was promoted by a monarch, Kalākaua of the Kingdom of Hawaii, as a symbol of his culture. And, finally, the acoustic guitar can be found on the stages of the dingiest country music dive bar and the most ornate concert hall dedicated to performances of classical music; in both places musicians are likely to show their virtuosic command of the instrument as they sing an ornate verse about new (or lost) love. While the specific possibilities of an instrument—or any sounding technology—influence how people interact with it, we cannot reduce music to its technologies nor explain everything about music through its technologies.

Media

Music happens in time—our experience of that time is an always-dynamic undertaking. Put differently, we might say that music creates a sense of time. A three-minute chart-topping hit is boring when we listen to it for the eighth time on a six-hour road trip. When it comes back on the radio while we are waiting for a coffee to brew on the way to work, we linger on every second. In this example, music mediates time. It literally fills up 180 seconds. It makes those 180 seconds feel slow when we're bored; when we're nostalgic (or stressed) it makes them feel long. It transmits a beat into our body: we can count the beats that shape its flow. When we remember other times we have heard the song, it references time past. Maybe we sing the song's melody later: we cling to time, reshaping it on our own terms. When we listen together with someone else, we share time. This special relationship to time is what media scholars highlight when they distinguish how sound mediates—sound as media—from, for example, print or other visual representations. This is a more abstract definition of the concept of media than the one that I will focus on here—which concerns the materials that mediate music—but it is important to consider it, not least because it calls back to the practice of questioning our listening with which I opened. What kinds of experiences of time does listening introduce into your life over one day?

As time-specific media, sound media, especially recordings, draw attention to the special function of sound. A recording can capture a melody so we can hear it again. Recording cuts off a sound from its source and original context: sound can travel around the world as an mp3 file. We can own it, copy it, and share it. But sound recordings are not themselves necessarily stable objects: a studio engineer can manipulate a sound recording—stretch it to make it longer or speed it up—so we notice different details and dance to a different beat. From the edges of a dance floor, a DJ grabs a sample from one track, and builds a whole 40-minute groove out of it.

The history of sound recording is, in some ways, the history of the institutional study of world music. Some would argue that the discipline of ethnomusicology was made possible because of sound recording. Beginning in the late nineteenth century, sonic vibrations could be captured on physical materials from which they could be played back. First these grooves were encoded on wax. Later, in the twentieth century, they were translated through changing technologies of inscription onto shellac, vinyl, and magnetic tape. Each format was cheaper and more portable—making it easier to move sound—share (and sell)—it across the world. In the digital era, soundwaves are compressed into mp3s—zeroes and ones—that we can send as email attachments or upload to the cloud.

If there is anything we learn by questioning listening, it is that listening is not a passive activity. Sound recording has not just expanded access to music, its technologies have provoked new approaches to listening and have shaped the formation of new musical subcultures. Recording begets new ways of hearing music live. Marié Abe discusses an extraordinary example of this when she introduces Japanoise in her chapter on Japan (see *Excursions*, Chapter 6). This music is ear-shatteringly loud, its creators almost abrasively asking people not to listen. These DIY artists, from the 1970s to the present, manipulate recordings, often those from punk and experimental bands in North America. Focused listening prompted them to hear the music on their own terms: they distort it beyond recognition with their own music technologies (pedals, amplifiers) to overload their sound systems with information—a technique that generates the scorching sounds of "feedback" that is especially debilitating in the small spaces of underground clubs. Japanoise is part social experiment, part artistic provocation, part sensational event. Eventually, its subcultural sounds became popular in North America, producing a kind of metaphorical feedback loop for Japanoise's circulation.

Summary

Does the seeming omnipresence of sound recording(s) mean we are all ethnomusicologists now: do we listen to more different music or to music more differently than people 100 years ago? Do we share more listening habits if our sound media are more similar? One myth about access to sound recording is that the music industry dampens artistic creativity. This is a variation on the fear of cultural homogenization in the age of what have often been called "new media"—television, the internet. A simple rebuttal to this claim of increasing sameness might be to trace the global examples of hip-hop across *Excursions*. (It's worth remembering here the density of mediation and technological manipulation upon which hip-hop is based: the art form has its origins in the manipulation of vinyl records to scratch beats and create grooves as well as the careful curation of mixtapes, to be circulated hand-to-hand, copied for free, and remixed on cassettes.) Hip-hop's global circulation is certainly a result of the cultural and economic power of the United States in the twentieth and twenty-first centuries, but its local iterations do not only vary in terms of musical technique and aesthetic value. They often—domestically, too—articulate hostility toward imperialism, toward the systemic racism of the United States, and toward other institutions of control and power.

However, these anxieties about ubiquity and connectivity share a premise that we ought to take seriously. In the twenty-first century, making and listening to sound recordings seems easier than ever before. Many of us communicate consistently through smartphones—which connect us to the internet, enable us to make a phone call, let us make music on apps, and allow us to make sound recordings. This single device combines the possibilities of the telephone, Walkman, radio, and television (all technologies that would be called "old media" now, even if they were once new) in a portable fashion that sometimes gives us the illusion that the world—including the world of music and sound—is at our fingertips. We, as budding scholars of world music, might perceive ourselves to be in the moment of sound technologies' apotheosis.

Excursions in World Music, however, challenges you to think about how you get access to this music. Recall a takeaway from the questioning listening exercise with which we began. Remarking on the space and privilege music receives in our lives, I wrote: we set aside time for it and, sometimes unconsciously, orchestrate how it resonates. Studying communication, technology, and media, means thinking about access in terms of what technologies and materials bring music to life. One musical example, in the chapter by Chérie Ndaliko, reveals how politically-charged musicians raise the challenging paradoxes inherent in digital culture, which depends on scarce raw materials while also creating greater access to communication (see *Excursions*, Chapter 8). Angélique Kidjo's *Remain in Light* protests the resource wars fought in Congo, their exploitation of human lives in Africa to the benefit of technological progress. In song, she criticizes tech companies who subsidize nation-states' military intervention, as they scramble for access to the rare ore, coltan, that is essential to the capacitors that make your cell phone work. As Kidjo sings "Take a look at these hands," over and over in a scattershot rhythm, it's unclear if she's asking the listener to take a look at themselves—or if she's simply, as the lyrics suggest, calling out the "Government Man" for predictable exploitation. Know that you are a part of this, she implies; remember to question the power structures that configure your life.

Our cell phones, *Excursions in World Music* would like to suggest, are sound technologies that provide access and exploit at once. There is no clear evidence of progress here, but neither simply fodder for suspicion. Music, broadly, offers the opportunity to take a look at ourselves and how we relate to others: to think about communication. The meanings we derive from music are political, aesthetic, ideological, and communal. Sound recordings do not merely cast these possibilities on a global scale. Sometimes it is those unremarkable, accidental recordings—never commercially released, maybe from one's youth or of a loved one—that we hold as intimate and share to create intimacy. When we question, we do not only challenge our ears, we learn and yearn to understand the knowledge listening transmits, the feelings sound technologies impart, and how we can and want to share these objects—that is, the ways in which sound and music communicate.

8

MUSICAL LABOR, MUSICAL VALUE

Jim Sykes

"No, you will not major in music."
(Our parents)

Following Sri Lanka's devastating 2004 tsunami, I interned at the United Nations' Office of the Special Envoy for Tsunami Recovery, headed by former U.S. President Bill Clinton. (For the record, I never met him, but I did deliver his mail.) At one point, I found myself in a bureaucrat's office, both of us in suits and ties, talking about corporate contributions to the tsunami relief effort. He found out that I was in the midst of coursework for a Ph.D. in ethnomusicology. Worried that I might be considering leaving a life in music to work for a government agency or non-governmental organization (NGO) dedicated to social activism, he looked silently out the window at the skyscrapers for an awkward amount of time. "I was an artist once," he said, miserably. Then he swiveled his chair towards me and said not to give up on music, that I'd *do more for good for the world* as a musician.

A couple years later, during the final phase of Sri Lanka's terrible war (1983–2009), I was in the country interviewing a musician who had performed at several "concerts for peace." The point of the concerts was to bring musicians together from the two ethnic groups perceived to be on either side of Sri Lanka's war in order to promote peace between the communities. I asked her if the concerts had worked. She shrugged and replied, "do we have peace?" The implication was clear: if I wanted actual social change, I should work for a government agency or NGO. Indeed, Sri Lanka's war *did* end about a year after that interview—not due to the efforts of musicians or NGOs but because of a government bombing campaign that resulted in the deaths of the rebel leader, most of the remaining rebel fighters, and thousands of innocent civilians.

My parents always encouraged me to follow my passion for music. From the requisite piano lessons as a child, to an awful year honking away at clarinet in elementary school, to my passion for drums that resulted in a drum set located just above my parent's bedroom during high school, they encouraged me despite my tendency to disturb them at any hour. But this began to change after college.

Once I started touring with bands, they became genuinely skeptical. How will you make a living playing music? Why would you want to be on the road so much? Is it a sustainable way to make a living? Why not be a music journalist? Don't all musicians do drugs? My older brother—an avid music fan and great guitarist who happens to be an investment banker living in a large mansion in Connecticut—provided another model.

A few years ago, at a dinner party at my brother's house held for a special occasion, I sat next to a distant relative, herself a successful businesswoman. Sitting on the beautiful veranda outside my brother's home, she found it appropriate to begin our conversation by saying, "I bet you could never afford this on a music teacher's salary." The truth is, I never cared to live in a mansion. I have had the strange fate of being middle class from a rich town (my father was a high school history teacher, my mother worked as a photo editor), doing fieldwork in some poor locations (such as rural Sri Lanka), then going to family events at a mansion. I had heard this kind of comment before, so I wasn't surprised. But it still stung, perhaps because I hadn't seen this woman since childhood and I was amazed she thought it appropriate to say this to a virtual stranger. It reminded me of a number of classic drummer jokes that poke fun at how since drumming is economically unfeasible—the point is never left in doubt—drummers are societally worthless: "What do you call a drummer who breaks up with his girlfriend? Homeless." "How do you get a drummer off your porch? Pay him ten bucks for the pizza." The fact these jokes are about men probably just reflects the unfortunate reality that there have been far fewer women drummers. "What do you say to a drummer in a three-piece suit? Will the defendant please rise?" "What is the difference between a drummer and a savings bond? One will mature and make money."

I am still not living in a mansion, but perhaps the joke's on them. Having ridden the wave of many bands (some miserable failures and some surprisingly somewhat successful), I was lucky enough to achieve tenure as a professor of music—a stability gained, I should emphasize, through my scholarship *about* music rather than music performance. My brother, still paying the mortgage on that mansion, continues to navigate the stressful, ever-fluctuating market. My parents now tell me they are more worried about him than me, despite the still-severe difference in our bank accounts. "Well that's a change," I told them.

Music's Relevance, Music's Sustenance

I think the above stories capture something essential about our era, and not just its economic inequality. Namely: we seem incapable of deciding whether music is worthless or if it is the most important thing in the world. While some of us seem heavily invested in defending one side of this debate or the other, many of us act as though both are true simultaneously (somehow, a middle point between the two poles never seems to be an option).

Musicians are frequently caught in the middle—perhaps it is more accurate to say they are ignored or exploited. Consider, for example, the world of musical philanthropy. The founder of Target, Robert J. Ulrich, loves music so much that he founded a museum of musical instruments in Phoenix, Arizona, that cost $250 million to build. One of the founders of Microsoft, Paul Allen, founded the Experience Music Project (now the Museum of Pop Culture) in Seattle, famous for its annual pop music conference and programs like a battle of the bands for musicians under the age of 21. The building was designed by the famed architect Frank Gehry; the entire project cost about $240 million dollars. The Rock & Roll Hall of Fame in Cleveland, which opened in 1995, is marketed as a major tourist attraction for that city and cost $84 million dollars. While I appreciate that these rich individuals and cities are valuing music, I often wonder if it would have been better to give those millions of dollars to living, breathing musicians. I've learned in my own music career that while many people make money off musicians—wonderful people who are booking agents, record labels, public relations firms, music websites like Pitchfork, employees at Spotify, and so on—it is ridiculously difficult for even many successful musicians to stay afloat. Back in the late 2000s, for example, reports came out that the members of one of the most successful indie bands of that era, Grizzly Bear, were each making about $30,000 a year—if that's what success looks like, what about everyone else? It has been estimated that, at current rates, it would take around 400,000 plays on Spotify to reach something approaching minimum wage, but this money would likely need to be divided between multiple band members, a record label, and a rights organization like the American Society of Composers, Authors, and Publishers (ASCAP). For most musicians, the number of streams needed for minimum wage is in the millions. While *Business Insider* and *Forbes* routinely report how much musicians like Taylor Swift make in a given year, there is a lack of data on what average (professional touring and recording) musicians make—I suspect it is well below minimum wage. Though I have no data on this, I suspect it is probably easier to make a living working at the ticket booth at the Rock & Roll Hall of Fame than to be a professional touring musician with a somewhat-decent fanbase (at least the ticket booth vendor probably has a salary and health insurance).

I don't want to be all doom-and-gloom here: the digital age has opened up many new and exciting avenues for sustaining oneself musically that did not exist fifteen or even five years ago. In some ways, things are much better now than during the period described above (late 2000s/early 2010s). As digitization has become the new normal, musicians are finding ways to thrive in our gig economy, while certain kinds of musical labor—such as film scoring, producing, or being a DJ—have grown in exciting ways.

Yet I suggest the system remains rotten at its core and that the problem extends far beyond music to other types of creative labor. A good comparison is with writers. The UK newspaper *The Guardian* reported in 2018 that median earnings for professional writers had declined 42% since 2005 to just under £10,500 a year, coming out to £5.73 per hour on a 35-hour work week. The median income for all published authors in the U.S. from writing-related activities was $6,080 according to a study by the Author's Guild.

Musical Labor in and beyond Capitalism

All this raises a lot of questions. Is it fair for creative labor to be so devalued? Why does this happen? If some creative livelihoods are more sustainable than others, which are they? Has the digital age made creative livelihoods more or less possible? Who is to blame for the difficulty of supporting oneself through the arts—is it artists themselves, societal values, brute economic realities, the internet, and/or other factors? Is it possible to make creative livelihoods more plausible and respected?

These questions are not easily answerable, and exploring them in detail is well beyond the bounds of this chapter. Nevertheless, I will try to make some headway here on a few of them pertaining to musical labor. In what follows, I argue that our devaluing of musical labor is due in part to how art objects are defined in our modern world as either mere entertainment—and thus seemingly of less value to society than (say) being a doctor or lawyer—or as having social value due to art's ability to *critique* or *reflect* society rather than as an activity that *creates* and *sustains* society. While this understanding applied to music is intimately entangled with the placement and spread of music in global capitalism, I show in the next section that it emerged in large part through a specifically Western understanding of musical labor and value. Note that my aim here is not simply to understand this Western framing of musical labor, nor to claim it is globally normative, but rather to pivot from it to consider diverse examples of musical labor around the world culled from *Excursions in World Music*—examples that demonstrate alternative ways of being, belonging, valuing, and sustaining oneself through music.

I suggest it is only by realizing that we benefit from musicians as everyday workers at least as much as we do from musician celebrities that we can begin to create more respect for musicians and thus change the perception that they contribute little to our society at a basic level. Maybe this is naïve, but I hope that such a change in perspective could lead to a revolution in the perceived value of musical labor and thus force us to consider paying musicians and respecting them more. One way to begin this project is by putting ourselves in musicians' shoes—*Excursions in World Music* provides myriad examples. Note that I am *not* urging us to go back to a romanticized notion of premodern musical labor—musicians have often been unjustly derided and put in a subordinate place in the social hierarchy. Nevertheless, musicians have *also* often been tasked with important, fundamental roles in creating and sustaining society. I suggest that looking at different forms of musical labor around the world will demonstrate that the failure of many capitalist societies to value and create well-paying, sustainable jobs for musicians is more a fault of the capitalist imagination than it is the fault of musicians themselves. Perhaps I can convince some of you to devise new ways to sustain musical livelihoods in a capitalist system that appears to value musical celebrities at the expense of everyone else.

Musical Efficacy in Western Thought

The word "epiphenomenal" refers to an action or object caused by something else that does not cause other things in turn: the Merriam-Webster dictionary defines it as "a secondary phenomenon accompanying another and caused by it specifically."[1] To some of you this may seem odd, but people often act as though music is an epiphenomenon: they feel music emerges from certain causes without thinking that music *in turn* causes things in society. To put this another way, for those who hold this view, music is the result of societal actions but does not actually construct society. I believe this is one reason music often appears (generously) as a special form of labor (a rare and unique profession) or (less generously) as "not a real job": music is often performed on a concert stage at night, after most of the audience has had a full work day, and is viewed as blowing off steam.

Consider what the famous nineteenth-century theorist Karl Marx (1973 [1939]: 305) wrote about the musician's "unproductive labor":

> *Productive labour* is only that which produces *capital*. Is it not crazy ... that the piano maker is a *productive worker*, but not the *piano player*, although obviously the piano would be absurd without the piano player? But this is exactly the case. The piano maker reproduces *capital*; the pianist only exchanges his labour for revenue. But doesn't the pianist produce music and satisfy our musical ear, does he not even to a certain extent produce the latter? He does indeed: his labour produces something; but that does not make it *productive labour* in the *economic sense*; no more than the labour of the madman who produces delusions is productive.

Despite Marx's status as the premier critic of capitalism, I think his perspective is widespread among those who live and work in capitalism. But as I have shown above, even in the paradigmatic example of the touring musician, a whole industry has grown up around music—so music *is* productive of capital (at the time I'm writing this, Spotify is valued at 8 billion dollars, very little of it going to musicians). Unlike the piano, music appears ephemeral and immaterial. But as zeros and ones sent as mp3s or as a musician performing in public, music materializes in many different ways that are commodified—and these commodities generate attention, capital, and related forms of labor.

Music's epiphenomenal status was taken for granted even by many scholars of music for about two hundred years. In the late eighteenth and early nineteenth centuries, European music critics became frustrated with what they viewed as the social obligations of composers: even the world's famous classical composers such as Bach, Mozart, and Beethoven had to fulfill commissions paid for by

75

wealthy donors, and they had to perform or compose for church services, state events, and other social functions. Such professional obligations appeared to limit the time they could spend on art for art's sake, and it appeared to compromise their music's quality by forcing them to cater to an audience. Music critic E.T.A. Hoffman famously derided these obligations, believing musicians should devote themselves solely to their musical works. He wrote that,

> The genuine artist lives only for the work, which he understands as the composer understood it and which he now performs. He does not make his personality count in any way. All his thoughts and actions are directed towards bringing into being all the wonderful, enchanting pictures and impressions the composer sealed in his work with magical power.
>
> (Quoted in Goehr 1992: 1)

Hoffman published a review of Beethoven's Fifth Symphony in 1810 where he claimed that instrumental music is more powerful than art that relies on language or images. This came to be called "absolute music." Over the course of the nineteenth century in Europe, the Romantic movement theorized music as an expression of the inner workings of the composer's soul (perhaps as a channeling of God and/or the composer's genius).

You may feel very little attachment to nineteenth-century Europe, but it is important to realize that these notions of music—as related to the solitary genius, music's perceived transcendence from society, and the notion that music is a specialized activity that requires much training—have all shaped our current skepticism about the social value of music. I suggest these notions lie at the heart of music and capitalism. For example, when you log on to Spotify, you are presented with the impression that music is always and just naturally a personal, intimate endeavor that relates to or produces your mood. Rather than define the "musical work" as a musician's ability to create social ties between people, Spotify defines music as "the soundtrack to your life" (a phrase that makes it sound like music is auxiliary and accompanying rather than constitutive of life). Music is defined as being about who *you* are rather than about how you connect with others, and about forming or enhancing your mood while you do other, seemingly more important, "actual" tasks. This hyper-personalization and obscuring of the social is fundamental to contemporary capitalism (often referred to as neoliberalism) and, I suggest, is a reason why many people in our society feel lonely and depressed.

Expanding Music's Powers

When I was writing up my Sri Lankan research, I became fascinated by that quote from Hoffman above, which made it into my book (Sykes 2018: 55). This is because the musicians I studied with in Sri Lanka find value in their social service to others—in their musical *work* rather than their musical work, if you get what I mean. I studied with a caste called the Beravā—a hereditary group of ritualists, drummers, singers, dancers, mask-makers, and astrologers active in southern and southwestern Sri Lanka (see Excursions, Chapter 2). The Beravā belong to Sri Lanka's Sinhala ethnic majority; they identify as Theravada Buddhist (the oldest form of Buddhism that is also prevalent in mainland Southeast Asia—Myanmar, Thailand, Laos, and Cambodia). Historically, the Beravā were village doctors. You'd visit one if you had an illness and they might prescribe herbal medicine, tell you to visit a modern hospital, or prescribe a large-scale healing ritual. Their drumming, singing, and dancing are classified as Ayurvedic medicine, the traditional medicinal system prevalent throughout South Asia. For the Beravā, their artistic practices are not expressions of their inner self or soul, for Buddhists do not believe in a "soul" the way (say) Christians do. Nor do the Beravā "compose" their music, for their traditions are passed down, with some pieces composed by the gods themselves. The Beravā's artist practices are conceptualized as gifts offered to the Buddha and deities in the hopes that the deities will protect them from natural disasters and illnesses. Unlike so much music in our modern world—where music is about the ego of the performer, or a product we use to tailor our identity and sustain or produce our moods (such as through Spotify playlists)—music for the Beravā is about respecting and helping others. But as I discovered while writing my book, even in Sri Lanka the forces of nationalism have portrayed Beravā music and dance as being about the ethnic identity of Sri Lanka's Sinhala Buddhist community rather than viewing music as a kind of medicine. My own drum teacher, for example, laments that Beravā drumming and dance had been placed in schools of the arts rather than medical schools.

Reframing Musical Labor and Value

The Beravā, like hereditary musicians in many societies (e.g., India and Korea) were traditionally placed on the bottom of the social hierarchy. Hereditary musicians have often been exploited by the upper castes/classes—capitalism is certainly not solely to blame for musicians' precarity. One example is in South India, where the outcaste Paraiyars (now called Dalits) had to (and in some cases, still do) play at upper-caste funerals and live in their own separate ghettoes or *cheris*. Sometimes such encounters between castes/classes facilitated an outright appropriation of the cultural practices of the lower-status group. One well-known example from South India occurred in the early twentieth century, when some upper-caste women ostensibly wanted to help the devadasis—the temple dancers who were wedded to a god and danced for him in a Hindu temple—by outlawing being a devadasi (which they viewed as facilitating prostitution) but "saving" their dance. Many scholars now believe the devadasis were unfairly maligned and their dances appropriated and transformed by the upper-caste women, who named the new version of the dance Bharata Natyam.

Not all such exchanges between social classes were negative, though—much as one might find both unsavory and exciting transformations of hip-hop as it moved from African-American communities around the United States and the world. In his chapter on Korea (see *Excursions*, Chapter 5), Joshua Pilzer notes that the improvisational chamber music called sinawi in the late nineteenth and early twentieth centuries brought together female gisaeng and male gwangdae performers to make "shamanist music in chamber settings for rural bureaucrats, aristocrats, and literati." In this way, Pilzer says, they "came to influence and be influenced by elite culture." All this is to say that traditional musical labor functioned much like musical labor today: people from different walks of life heard each other, encounters that sometimes facilitated harmonious engagements between people and at other times facilitated negativity and/or acts of cultural appropriation. Music is always transforming, as music that emerged in one context is repurposed for another. These caveats aside, I want to provide some brief examples here of how music traditionally played a role in economic and social life through an emphasis on collectivity, institutions, and respect for elder teachers as well as a belief that not all musical knowledge should be free. I suggest such examples provide a useful contrast for how music is understood within global capitalism.

Communal Labor, Human–Nonhuman Relations, and Personal Transformation

Joshua Pilzer notes that the Korean percussion and dance genre pungmul ("wind objects") began as part of rural ceremonies to bless houses, crops, villages, and events as well as to accompany and encourage rural work, such as the planting of rice sprouts and paddies (see *Excursions*, Chapter 5). It was also used to fundraise for village projects, temples, and other institutions. Pungmul is associated with traditional Korean farming culture. We can see from this example that music might be associated with a break from labor (such as farming), while also being a kind of work (fundraising).

Korean shamanism was the wellspring from which many forms of Korean traditional music emerged, and pungmul—associated also with certain shaman rituals and masked dance dramas—is no exception. As Pilzer notes, Korean shamanism is a type of animism, meaning it "holds that matter is imbued with a complex pantheon of spirits." Shamans are either possessed by spirits or act as intermediaries, and most shamans are women; in the ecstatic tradition, where they are possessed by spirits, they "often wear traditional men's clothing, as they are often possessed by male spirits." Pilzer notes that shamans seek to heal or mediate in response to crises, and this is not a moribund tradition of irrelevance to modern society: he lists the Asian financial crisis of 1997, the suicide of former President Roh Moo-hyun (No Mu-hyeon) in 2009, and the sinking of the Sewol Ferry in 2014 as contemporary examples. A shaman performance is *collective*, featuring responsorial singing and shouting (vocal interjections called *chuimsae*); after purifying the ritual space, a "road" is created along which the spirits travel to the ceremony and back; and the shamans "invite, receive blessings and advice, entertain and send off spirits, in descending hierarchical order; and feed and ward off evil spirits." Shaman rituals require music, and the hourglass drum *janggo* is requisite.

There are a number of things I'd like you to take from this example. First, Pilzer notes that shaman rituals are about "transformation—of time, feeling, content, and so on—especially emotion, or spirit." A core aspect of the rituals is to transform "isolation into unity, and sorrow into exhilaration and joy." Of course, music still does this today, but I believe we tend to be less focused on its *collective* transformative qualities and more focused on its relationship to personal identity and individual mood. The releasing of social tension and the loosening of social rules, which Pilzer also attributes to Korean shaman rituals, can of course be associated with modern rock, pop, and EDM concerts and festivals. But I suggest we tend to conceptualize those as entertainment, as blowing off steam, rather than as a fundamental way to collectively grapple with and transform crises or trauma into rebirth and joy.

Musical Secrets and Respect for Elders

Another hallmark of our modern world is the notion that information "wants to be free." We tend to believe we must have easy access to everything—all knowledge should be on Wikipedia, all films on Netflix, all music on Spotify. Such a belief is a radical transformation of traditional knowledge systems in a way that, to my mind, foregrounds the importance of the individual consumer rather than the importance that certain kinds of knowledge have for a society or the people who have devoted their lives to promoting and upholding it. It also devalues the collective *power* of musical knowledge, which has historically made much musical knowledge a heavily guarded secret.

Take, for instance, the way that musical knowledge is traditionally passed down throughout South Asia (see *Excursions*, Chapter 2). In Hindustani (North Indian) and Carnatic (South Indian) classical music alike, learning music traditionally required years of apprenticeship to a guru, who revealed certain musical skills and ragas only after the student's seriousness and devotion to the guru and music were apparent. In my chapter on South Asia, I describe the legendary story of Allauddin Khan, a foremost exponent of the sarod (lute) in early twentieth-century North India. Khan's story appears to be true, but it is also the kind of story that is easily mythologized. As someone who ran away from home as a child to pursue music, and then ran away from his wife upon being married, according to legend, Khan waited at the entrance to the court of Rampur for months before threatening suicide if he could not learn music from the legendary court musician Wazir Khan. Even then, the story goes, Allauddin Khan was not allowed to play for the guru for several years, as students were expected to soak up the guru's music simply from being around, while putting in hours of practice and doing chores for the guru. Hindustani and Carnatic musicians alike are known for broadcasting how devoted they are to music, particularly to grueling practice sessions. Another example from North India is of the tabla drummer Ustad Ahmed Jan Thirakwa, who (according to ethnomusicologist Dan Neuman) would tie his long hair up to the ceiling, so that when he fell asleep it would jerk him awake and he could keep practicing.

Sonic Efficacy

While these examples are extreme, it is important to realize why musical knowledge was so guarded. Traditionally throughout South Asia, music had (and in many ways, still has) efficacy. One could say musical secrets are akin to a chef's recipe and it is in the interest of the musician for business purposes to not give such secrets away. But as we saw with the case of the Beravā above, music in South Asia has long been associated with the traditional medicinal system Ayurveda (and with the Muslim medicinal system called Unani) and is ascribed certain powers. One famous story in Hindustani music is about how the legendary Mian Tansen (1500–1586), singer in the court of the Mughal Emperor Akbar, taught his daughter how to sing Raga Malhar (believed to cause rain) after the Emperor's scheming courtiers plotted to kill Tansen by forcing him to sing Raag Deepak (believed to cause fire). Beliefs in the efficaciousness of raags—performed at specific times of day or night, and specific seasons—long characterized Hindustani music. Ethnomusicologist Katherine Schofield has shown that Muslim writers during India's Mughal period believed melancholy was caused by an excess of the humor black bile, and this could be cured by music.

One realm where traditional investments in sound-as-power persists is funerals. (Perhaps people are willing to think of music as mere entertainment during life, but when it comes to the dead, better to not take any chances.) In South Indian funerals, some Paraiyars (Dalits) still play the parai drum to drive away evil spirits as a soul leaves a body. Similarly, an old Korean ritual that Joshua Pilzer describes as part of the rich legacy of Southwestern shamanism in Korea is the cleansing funeral ritual (sikkim gut) of Jindo Island, which begins "in the early evening and lasts until morning, proceeding through myriad formalized steps that facilitate the deceased's passage to the next world and help the living say goodbye." Musical efficacy continues to be more widespread in the modern world than is typically recognized, and this continues to shape what kinds of musical knowledge is shared. I found in Sri Lanka that I was not allowed to learn many drum patterns because, if performed incorrectly, it could lead to calamity: for if the job of the musician is to give music to the gods to protect your community from natural disasters such as drought and pestilence, offering it incorrectly (or not at all) could actually *cause* those problems. In South India, certain kinds of music must be played when the icon of a deity is taken out of the temple and wheeled around in a chariot. This is not simply a question of honoring the deity but that the deity is listening and could get mad if not given the proper offerings.

It is of course easy to deride such notions as premodern superstitions. Who would claim today that someone suffering from a medical issue should forego a hospital for a ritual of drumming and dance? And yet, in many ways, modern science has confirmed what we already know—sound is physically transformative and affects mind, body, and mood. The field of music therapy is growing. While one can find out about any given raag these days via the internet, I suggest that the system involving carefully guarding and slowly doling out of musical knowledge is still the norm in South Asian musics. Ethnomusicologists have noted similar circumstances elsewhere, such as Thailand, where ethnomusicologist Deborah Wong (2001) found that Thai classical music is considered like a pyramid, where only students undergoing long apprenticeship to a guru—who is worshipped in a ceremony called the *wai khru*—gain access to knowledge about the most esteemed pieces. Sonic efficacy, in other words, is a core reason for the historic tendency to guard esteemed musical knowledge.

Local Histories and Collectivities: Respecting Wedding Musicians and Other Tales of Generosity, Gender, and Heroism

An example of a persisting, older form of musical sociality at the local level is found in the sung poetry traditions Richard Jankowsky describes in the Middle East and North Africa (see *Excursions*, Chapter 3). He notes that the pre-Islamic Arabic *qasida* (an improvised vocal piece based on classical Arabic poetic form of the same name) is still highly valued, and that female poet-singers are hired for weddings to sing such "songs of passion, fertility, and collective history." Jankowsky points out that epic singers may "create hours-long performances by reworking verses from an enormous corpus of memorized verses."

Another example he provides is the sung poetry of the Bedouins, the nomadic, desert-dwelling peoples found in North Africa. The singers traditionally narrated history, conveyed news of recent events, and carried interpersonal messages, while promoting individual sentiments like love and broader cultural ideals like generosity, honor, and heroism. One epic poem, the *Sīrat Banī Hilāl*, recounts the Bedouins' migration from Arabia westwards into Tunisia. Unfortunately, such epic singers today are sometimes viewed derogatorily as beggar-poets, a reputation they try to evade through their rebab, the bowed instrument that signifies heroism and the warriors described in their epic. Finally, Jankowsky notes the famous ethnography of female Berber singers by the anthropologist Lila Abu-Lughod (2016 [1986]), who found that Berber women used sung poetry for expressing "veiled sentiments" about love, marriage, family relationships, and society. Women professional singers traditionally sang in groups at Berber weddings, a genre called 'aiṭa, which recalls the deeds of heroes and extols the virtues of rural Berber society, while taking license with traditional gender codes by "sanctioning erotic images, the verbal abuse of unfit suiters, and social critique sometimes directed at government policy."

This notion of the musician as epic bard continues to be played out today—one could probably find ways to think of Kanye West, Kendrick Lamar, or Beyoncé in much the same terms. I believe the difference is that the individuals described above are locals, singing about issues affecting a local community (even if their themes resonate broadly by being about fundamental human emotions), in public forums where people of all ages from the community gather (such as weddings). I might also add that at many weddings today, DJs are a bit of an afterthought; but in many societies around the world, musicians sustained themselves economically and gained much respect from playing at weddings.

Musical Collectivity and Joy within Capitalism

Reading the above you could think there is a sharp dichotomy between pre-modern and capitalist forms of music-making, with the former associated with community/collectivity and the latter with the individual/isolation. But we all know that community-building through music occurs in capitalism. Here I wish to emphasize that such community-building may happen in ways that fall outside the typical music festivals and concert venues we associate with music in capitalism. One example from *Excursions* is the Japanese genre *chindon-ya*, described by Marié Abe (see *Excursions*, Chapter 6). Starting in the late nineteenth century, chindon-ya groups were hired by local businesses to "circulate through the neighborhood streets and attract attention by playing popular tunes to draw listeners into social interactions." The genre began, then, as an early form of advertising, in the days before radio, television, and internet. But chindon-ya groups don't play jingles. Rather, as Abe notes, they make a "sales pitch" through conversations with passersby who are drawn out onto the streets by chindon-ya's instrumental music. Abe points out that even as radio and television proliferated in Japan in the 1950s and 1960s, chindon-ya was still "ubiquitous in the everyday soundscape," though the music was often "sounds to be overheard from afar" rather than listened to up close or with close attention. Chindon-ya, a transnational hybrid practice that combines Japanese and Western musics, was influenced in part by the tradition of Western military brass bands. Nowadays, hearing the genre may cause pangs of nostalgia. Perhaps surprisingly, some of the groups have achieved financial success, and some rock, jazz, and experimental groups in Japan have taken up the "chindon-ya aesthetic."

Abe's book (2018) on chindon-ya emphasizes that the genre's focus on physical (rather than virtual) sociality seems at odds with the individualism and isolationism inherent in today's internet age. She says that chindon-ya harbors a "philosophy of sociality" (5) that runs counter to the modern world's tendency to produce "alienation as a collective social condition" (xx). As one chindon-ya musician, Hayashi Kōjirō, told her, "It's rare to find happy healthy people … you have to play so that the depressed want to come out" (xx). Whether you agree with this overarching understanding of the modern world as a collective of isolated and alienated individuals, we can all surely agree that we could use a little of chindon-ya's philosophy of sociality in our lives.

Conclusion

The above examples represent only a few of the forms of musical labor that differ from today's normative understanding of music (i.e., stars on Instagram, the next new thing on Soundcloud, giant tours and festivals, hit songs, and the like). I urge you not only to look for more examples of alternative forms of musical labor in *Excursions*, but also to think more often about how the sounds you encounter in your daily lives are produced by musicians who fall under the radar—including a broader sphere of music-related labor that includes recording engineers, film composers, music supervisors, booking agents, and so on.

As I stressed above, my aim here was not to over-romanticize older forms of musical labor nor to say that capitalism has only had a negative impact on musicians. I noted above that traditional social hierarchies often placed musicians at the bottom; and capitalism has allowed musicians to travel widely and gain followings that were unthinkable just a few hundred years ago. Nevertheless, I argued here that it could be useful to resurrect—or at least to better respect— certain aspects of musical labor and value from past generations. Examples I gave included the valuing of musical knowledge as something to be safeguarded and obtained through respecting elders; slowing down the transmission of musical knowledge; acknowledging the power of musical sound as transforming not just your mood but the world around you; emphasizing collective music-making and experiences over individual listening; reinvesting in musical labor in small-scale functional activities and celebrations, like weddings; and turning collective music-making towards the narration of local histories. Not only do such values still exist in some quarters, but I also showed in my last example that it is possible to promote some of them within capitalism. I suggest that reinvesting in such values could play some role towards a reevaluation of musical labor, generating better sustainability for performing musicians. The goal, in other words, is not to turn back the clock but rather to combine today's social mobility for musicians with a revaluation of collective and transformative music-making that, ideally, would generate more sustainable careers for musicians in the modern world.

Note

1 www.merriam-webster.com/dictionary/epiphenomenon.

References

Abe, Marié. 2018. *Resonances of Chindon-ya: Sounding Space and Sociality in Contemporary Japan*. Middletown, CT: Wesleyan University Press.

Abu-Lughod, Lila. 2016 [1986]. *Veiled Sentiments: Honor and Poetry in a Bedouin Society*. Berkeley, CA: University of California Press.

Goehr, Lydia. 1992. *The Imaginary Museum of Musical Works: An Essay in the Philosophy of Music*. New York: Oxford University Press.

Marx, Karl. 1973 [1939] *Grundrisse*. London: Penguin Classics.

Sykes, Jim. 2018. *The Musical Gift: Sonic Generosity in Post-War Sri Lanka*. New York: Oxford University Press.

Wong, Deborah. 2001. *Sounding the Center: History and Aesthetics in Thai Buddhist Performance*. Chicago, IL: University of Chicago Press.

9

MUSIC AND MEMORY

Lei Ouyang

Making music necessarily involves certain aspects of memory. What we learn as musicians is recalled and remembered in order to produce a note, read a musical score, or recall a piece from memory. Musicians of all levels develop such skills in highly specialized ways. For some, it may be entirely applied through practice and never intentionally or explicitly discussed. For others, these skills may be scrutinized and discussed as evidence of explicit intention and design. Similarly, listening to music also necessarily involves certain aspects of memory. As amateur and everyday listeners, our memory is activated through the music we encounter; be it a commercial jingle, children's song, song of worship, or pop song. As hearing individuals, we often recall and recognize music that we learned directly or indirectly in a previous context.

Listening to music can also activate a range of senses—often these are evocations of some type of memory. These memories can be individual and personal, or shared and collective. Take for example, *that one song* from *that one time*, a memory that is particular to you and only you—a memory of a specific place and time that is triggered or activated through music. Then take for example, *that one song* from *that one time*, a memory that is shared by the club you were a member of in high school; or that nearly an entire generation attributes to a particular social, political, or cultural moment.

How can an individual's memory be evoked through music? What about a collective memory that is shared by a group of people? What is happening in these moments of memory? I turn to four pairs of ideas as a way of starting to understand the range of possibilities concerning music and memory: performer and listener; individual and collective; content and process; and finally, past and present. I present these not as binaries but as broad areas within which to explore the full range and spectrum of possibilities for understanding the complexity of relationships and processes involved.

Performer and Listener

When we make music, we are calling upon some earlier memory. Take for example, a song that accompanies a children's hand-clapping game. The words, the tune,

85

and the hand movements were all learned at an earlier time. For a hand-clapping game, this could be part of one's informal enculturation (how we learn about the culture to which we belong) such as overhearing older siblings or relatives playing the games long before actually joining in. The process of recollecting, or remembering, is most likely not thought about in much detail, or with much attention—rather, the mind and body remember, and make the music. (These are complex processes, stated simply here, but closely researched by scholars in fields such as music cognition and neuroscience.) Now consider another example: a high school student singing as the featured soloist in the school musical. Once again, the production of lyrics and melody (the entire performance), is the result of learning and practice that took place before the performance. Even as the song unfolds, the musician is recalling the many hours of practice and rehearsal that preceded this performance: perhaps there were lessons with a vocal coach; maybe this singer listened diligently to recordings of other performances of this song; there might have been sessions sitting at a piano to learn the melody; and, of course, participation in the hours of rehearsal required to coordinate the accompaniment and stage directions. This musical moment would not be possible without memory—without memorization. But, when we say that this soloist memorized the song, it means much more than merely knowing the melody or the lyrics "by heart." It also means that the musician remembers having learned this material (remembers the mental and physical endeavor of "practice," that is), and recalls how it feels to "hit that note just right" (and that feeling is recalled from embodied memory).

Now consider the listener. A parent or older relative listening to the children singing and playing hand-clapping games may suddenly recall (remember) all the words from their own childhood despite the time that has since passed. Or perhaps they recall a memory of playing the games with friends during their own youth. Or, in the example of the high school musical, perhaps a student sitting in the audience has been listening to the soundtrack for the musical for the past two years and, though not a performer themselves, has developed deep associations connected with the music. Hearing the live performance may transport them to another time and place or conjure a particular emotion or a memory of a previous encounter with the music. The point here is that memory is significant for both the performer and the listener, yet in different ways. Further distinctions appear when we consider how memory works for an individual versus a group.

Individual and Collective

Throughout *Excursions in World Music* we have been exploring music as sound and music as culture; pushing beyond the notes themselves to also attend to the many meanings that are woven into and embedded within music. Music can evoke or occasion memories and emotions that are tied to these meanings. These meanings can be connected to an individual or shared by a broader group of people, such as members of a shared cultural group. In order to think a bit more about how this works for an individual, let's go back to the high school student sitting in the audience at the high school musical performance. What if that student experienced their first break-up later that night after attending the musical with their sweetheart and, as a result, for the rest of their life, whenever they hear that particular solo, the feelings of heartbreak surface even though the song has nothing to do with love or heartbreak? In this instance, the emotions from a particular moment that are embedded within the individual's memory are triggered by the music. Now, imagine the musical was a popular event shared by the graduating senior class that year. Fast forward to the 25-year reunion and, upon playing the soundtrack to the musical, the former classmates are excited to reminisce about memories from their senior year. Once again, the lyrics or content of the musical may be completely irrelevant in this moment of remembering, but for this collective group, the musical represents a shared moment in time, a shared history, that is once again, triggered by the music. These are but two examples of how music can facilitate the act, or process, of remembering in remarkably powerful ways.

Content and Process

Hearing individuals typically have some experience with the way that music can help facilitate the memorization of words or movements. For example, consider the way the alphabet song helps children learn the letters of the English alphabet; or how singing helps one remember religious scripture; or, in something such as hand-clapping games, how the accompanying songs actually help facilitate memorizing the associated hand movements. Music, then, can function as a mnemonic device. Once set to music, a set of words, phrases, or movements, is often significantly easier to remember.

But there is also the way that music helps evoke or becomes a catalyst for memory—the way that music can be a part of the process involved in remembering. The emotions and memories evoked upon hearing music, at times completely disconnected from the content, words, or melodies, of the music itself, are nevertheless driven by the sounds we are hearing and the associations they have for us. In these moments, memory is about the process of remembering, rather than about remembering particular content. Put another way, music can play an important role in triggering a memory precisely because of the ways we invest music with meaning and significance. How exactly these memories are triggered through music is of great interest to many scholars of music cognition, to psychologists, and to therapists working with dementia patients, to name just a few. Ethnomusicologists are also interested in the process of remembering through music, recognizing that the meanings of music are understood through context. Ethnomusicologists explore the contexts within which individuals or communities create, practice, perform, and listen to music, both in the past and in the present, studying processes such as those involved with music and memory in order to gain insights into communities, societies, cultures, and history.

Past in the Present

On the surface, memories, and the process of remembering, may seem to be about the past. And yet, when we remember the past, it is always from our position in the present. That is, the process of remembering is not exclusively about the past, but rather, a process of reflection *about* the past *from* the present. As a result, how we remember the past is not exclusively or objectively about the past, but is, instead, always filtered through the lens of the present. As such, processes of remembering will always be influenced by our present moment. For example, how does the present moment compare to the past? What are we choosing to remember? And more significantly, what are we choosing to forget, leave out, or skip over? Remembering our past is always a partial and selective process; a reconstructed idea of a time, a person, or a moment. What's happening in that process of reconstruction can tell us a lot about how one's present compares to one's past. Hearing a song from your childhood as a 25-year-old may bring about certain memories and emotions; but imagine that you, now 85 years old, hear the same song from your childhood and the memories and emotions that may be triggered through the music. Would you "hear" and "remember" the same thing? Although certain aspects of the memories may remain intact, the perspective that an 85-year-old, having lived long decades of life since childhood, brings to this exercise is different from that of their younger self. In a profound way, your 85-year-old self will "hear" your childhood from a very different vantage point than your younger selves would have been able to enjoy. Living with the accumulated experiences of a lifetime is certain to create a different relationship to childhood and thus lead to new or different emotions upon hearing that same song from childhood.

Moreover, music has a particularly productive way of enabling what my students often refer to as "time travel"—a process that brings you back to another time, place, emotion, and moment in life. And when one's present is drastically different from the past, music can act as an important connection to that distant, and perhaps otherwise irretrievable, past. One striking example can be found in moments of rupture. After moments of violence or trauma, perhaps war or genocide, people can be in need of reconciling themselves to a painful past in order to live fully in the present. Music can play an important role in such processes of remembering, helping to facilitate an otherwise impossible, or painful reconnection to earlier life experiences after such moments of rupture. In my own research on music from the Chinese Cultural Revolution, I have found that the period is a politically sensitive topic and indexes an emotionally (and at times physically) traumatic period for many who lived through those years. Talking about this time period can thus be a difficult conversation to get started, but I have observed that music can be an engaging way to facilitate such a discussion—once we start talking about music and the person begins to travel back in time, the conversation often opens up in new dimensions.

I turn now to three examples that help illustrate some of the complexities of music and memory I briefly introduced above. I begin with the story of erhu virtuoso Chen Jiebing's encounter with a piece of music from the Cultural Revolution that she had not heard in decades. Two further case studies explore the ways that music and memory work in folk music from Okinawa and in the practice of joiking among the Sámi.

"Shaoshan" (China and Taiwan)

Chen Jiebing's experiences with "Shaoshan," a piece for solo erhu and orchestra, not only provide insight into the period of the Cultural Revolution in China, but also shed light on a number of important processes involved in the relationship between music and memory (see *Excursions*, Chapter 4). First, Chen Jiebing was surprised to discover, upon hearing a recording in 2019, that she actually remembered most of a composition that she had not played or heard since the 1970s. Despite a gap of several decades the piece was still "in her fingers," as some musicians say. That is, there is a memory that is activated in performing music that is the result of careful training and practice, coupled with artistry and experience. What is significant to me is that Chen Jiebing may not have realized that she still had the ability to perform the piece after so many years—until she heard it again. The audio recording reactivated a memorized piece—that is, something that she had committed to memory. This phenomenon can also be explained in detail by psychologists and scholars working on music cognition. For our discussion here, I wonder what comes to your mind in terms of memory? Perhaps it is the one piece you learned early on in life on the piano, guitar, or another instrument? Or the lyrics to "that one song" that you played or listened to over and over again in your childhood or teenage years? Have you ever been surprised to find that you remember all the words to a song you have not heard in a while?

What exactly does Chen Jiebing remember when listening to a recording of "Shaoshan" after all these years, and why? Beyond the mechanical skill of being able to play the notes and phrases of the composition, there is also a layer of the emotions and memories linked to what it meant to perform the composition at that time in her life. Originally composed for the specific political and historical moment of the Cultural Revolution, "Shaoshan" was a composition meant to express commitment to the Chinese Communist Party and devotion to Chairman Mao Zedong. After all, the piece very intentionally participates in political propaganda—that is, the music is composed and disseminated with the specific function of supporting a political campaign and movement.

And yet, what does Chen Jiebing remember when listening to the recording today? Is it Mao? Is it socialist ideology? Certainly, that is a part of it that cannot be overlooked. But that is not the only dimension she remembers, for hearing this composition also creates a bridge—an aural connection to her youth. Hearing "Shaoshan" triggers memories of a formative time in her personal and musical development that are, because of the socio-political intensity of the Cultural Revolution and post-Cultural Revolution, disconnected from most of her adulthood and current everyday life. It is a way for her to revisit her youth through a physical recording, that offers her audible evidence of her own musical performance. And, as she shared with me, hearing this recording also grounds her memory and recollection in new ways. Whereas she previously had to imagine what she sounded like as a young performer, she can now hear herself on an actual audio recording. Chen Jiebing's memory is thus very much tied to her own individual experience and the meaning and emotion that she attaches to "Shaoshan."

"Hiyami Kachi Bushi" (Japan)

The song, "Hiyami Kachi Bushi," by contrast, illustrates a shared, or collective, memory that is evoked through music (see *Excursions*, Chapter 6). As Marié Abe writes: "Memories of the past are highly contested, with their repercussions continuing to inform the everyday lives of Okinawan people. Music is one of the cultural platforms where a distinct sense of Okinawan identity is expressed, questioned, and transformed." One can imagine a number of memories and emotions that might be evoked through the folk song. Starting with the sanshin, the three-string lute that commonly accompanies vocalists in songs such as "Hiyami Kachi Bushi," the instrument is distinctly and proudly *uchinanchu*, that is, Okinawan. Yet the history of the instrument is tied to musical and cultural exchange between the Ryukyu Kingdom and China; a fraught political relationship that played out across multiple historical eras. Similarly, the emotions and conviction of Taira Shinsuke and Yamanouchi Seihin's lyrics and melody signal complex memories of Okinawa. That is, memories of a homeland simultaneously full of beauty and tragedy. How can one song contain such contrasting images and emotions? What songs come to your mind that evoke memories of both joy and hardship?

"Hiyami Kachi Bushi" begins with the lines "Famed Okinawa/It's an island of treasure/gather your hearts into one and stand up," followed by "Let's rise up! Let's go for it!," and closes with "Falling seven times/but get up with determination/let our Okinawa be known to the world." The memories evoked through the lyrics alone signal a commemoration of the beauty of Okinawa and its people, in spite of the tragedy and hardships endured through the legacies of colonization, war, and other acts of violence. Such remembrance can be powerful for Okinawans both inside and outside of Okinawa. The lyrics, coupled, with music, provide a "cultural platform," as Abe writes, to make audible the history of Okinawa in beauty and suffering, but ultimately as a means of celebrating its potential. Here, a commemoration of the magnificence of an Okinawan past, can help facilitate a sense of empowerment and pride to negotiate the present, across the difficult terrain that lies between the past and the present.

"Eanan" (Music of Indigenous Peoples)

"Eanan," a song included on A Tribe Called Red's album *We Are the Haluci Nation*, features the Sámi tradition of joiks, or joiking. As Byron Dueck explains, the Sámi tradition of joiking evokes an animal, person, or aspect of nature in sung form (see *Excursions*, Chapter 12). Joiking a person, for example, is actually not limited to, or exclusively, a commemoration or memory of that person. It is, instead, an evocation of the spirit of that person in its broadest conception. The practice of joiking is simultaneously a performance of memory as content and memory as process; with the subject of the joik as the *content* of memory and the act of joiking as a *process* of memory.

Joiks and the process of joiking thus offer a compelling glimpse into the complex relationships between music and memory. They help us see that the process of remembering is not exclusively about the past but, as I discussed earlier, the process of remembering the past requires a present; a contemporary moment from which one is making a connection to some past. Learning about joiks and joiking provides the opportunity to sit in these moments and within these acts and processes of memory. How can we understand what is happening in these moments of remembering and commemoration? How can we understand the process of remembering that is happening in and through music? And how does the focus on such acts of remembering, and the processes of remembering, challenge our idea of what a memory is?

"Eanan" is a poignant example of how we can deepen our understanding of music and memory, content and process, and performative acts of remembering. The track is from an intertribal collaboration featuring Indigenous and non-Indigenous artists. The album as a whole represents an intentional commitment to incorporating various musical styles and traditions from Native American, First Nation, and Indigenous peoples around the world together with electronic dance music. Sámi artist Maxida Märak's joiking in "Eanan" could be understood as a call for Sámi community rights, or as a reference to an Indigenous tradition, or as a signal to non-Indigenous peoples to learn more about the Sámi and other Indigenous communities, or perhaps as a means of calling for all of the above. What is important to remember is that what is evoked, why, and how, will be different for every listener.

Music and Memory/Memory and Music

"Shaoshan," "Hiyami Kachi Bushi," and "Eanan" are just three examples to begin considering the complex relationships between music and memory. Who is remembering what and why? Is it a particular content commemorated in the music or lyrics? Or is there a memory attached to the music that is divorced from the content or design of the music itself but speaks to an earlier experience with the music? Are these memories particular to an individual or shared by a cultural group, cohort, or other group of individuals with shared experiences? What is it about music that facilitates an activation of senses? An activation that allows one to time travel, to resurrect a dormant set of words, or recall a specific memory, or re-experience a particular emotion? How does one's present shape our memory of the past?

91

Broadly speaking, ethnomusicologists seek to study music in context—within a cultural, and often, a historical context. Critical to this context are the people who are making and consuming this music. As we focus on this connection between people and music, then, we need to understand music's meaning and significance to individuals, and to communities; in a particular historical moment; and in the contemporary moment. When we consider memory, then we understand that such meaning and significance will shift depending on who is remembering what, when, and why. History is not fixed but dynamic, and this is because it is always a *re*-collection—a *re*-telling—from a new vantage point and with new stakes and concerns. Memories connected in, to, and through music will thus be activated in distinctly different ways depending on the context of the present. The very moment from which one remembers the past will inevitably shade and shape that memory and its meaning.

In conclusion, what might this discussion of music and memory mean to you? Take a look at the five most played tracks on your phone, or whatever device you use to listen to music. What memories come to mind when listening to these tracks? Are these memories specific to you and only you? Or are they shared with a group of friends or a larger community of which you are a member? Does the music help you remember a particular content, such as lyrics or a historic event? Or does the music help you time travel to another place or another moment in time through the process of remembering? How might your memories shift 10, 20, or 30 years from now when you hear this song again? Finally, consider opening up some conversations with elders in your family or community by accompanying them as they travel in time through music. How is this shared process of remembering unique to music? What more do you learn about their present through taking this journey with them to the past? Ultimately, as you ponder these various questions, how do you understand the connections between music, people, and culture in new or more nuanced ways?

INDEX

Abe, Marié 82
absolute music 76
Abu-Lughod, Lila 81
access to music 8, 61–3, 68–70;
    communication 64–5; media 67–8;
    technologies 63, 65–7
Africa: colonization 43; diaspora 53;
    sub-Saharan 15, 21, 29, 35
Afro-Caribbean identities 55
Afrofuturism 36–7
Algeria 12–13; national anthem 24–5
Anderson, Benedict 24
Anglophone popular music 3
apprenticeships 79, 81
Arab world 25
area studies 1–3
Area Studies Centres 2
Argentina, tango 44
Armenian diaspora 53
art for art's sake 76
art musics 3–4
arts, value 74
Ayerveda 80

Babylon 53–4
Bahamas 44; rake 'n' scrape 56
banjos 67
Bayreuth, Germany 26
Beravā 77
Blacking, John 20
Bohlman, Andrea F. 26
Bollywood film music 14
Bosavi people, Papua New Guinea 48
Brazil, *candomblé* 35–6
Burkina Faso 37–8
Byrne, David 4

Canada, national anthem 25
candomblé 35–6
capitalism 31–3, 42, 75, 76
Caribana, Toronto 59
Caribbean 44–5; diaspora, New York
    57–8; multiple origins 54; music
    traditions 55
champeta 37
children's games 85–6
chindon-ya 82
Chinese Cultural Revolution 88–9
Chinese migrants, Malaysia 57
classical music: composers 75–6; rituals 26
collectivity 78–9, 82
coloniality 2, 8, 29–30, 38, 38–9n1;
    capitalism 31–3, 42; control of
    knowledge 33–4; gender/sexuality
    14–15, impact of music 35–8; legacies
    5; music categorization 3–4, racial
    concerns 30–1
Columbia 32, 37
commodification 75
communication 8, 64–5
communitas 20
communities 9
community-building 82
content/process, memory 87, 91
context, listening 61–2
creative livelihoods 73, 74
Cree communities 48
creole musics 55–6
critical themes 4–7
crooners 14
Cuba, salsa 44–5
cultural appropriation 35
cultural aspects, coloniality 32, 34, 38, 42